THE Chivalrous MAN

CHIVALRY AND THE GODLY MAN

THE Chivalrous MAN

CHIVALRY AND THE GODLY MAN

GARY MILBY

WINEPRESS WP PUBLISHING

WinePress Publishing (PO Box 428, Enumclaw, WA 98022) functions only as book publisher. As such, the ultimate design, content, editorial accuracy, and views expressed or implied in this work are those of the author.

Unless otherwise noted, all Scriptures are taken from the King James Version of the Bible.

ISBN 1-57921-845-8
Library of Congress Catalog Card Number: 2006921677

TABLE OF CONTENTS

PREFACE

Men are subjected to many pressures over the course of their lifetimes that, for better or for worse, mold and shape the person they ultimately become. The criteria by which we are evaluated by our parents and families, by friends, by society, and especially by the women in our lives all predispose us to think, act, and behave in a manner that identifies us more by *what we do* than by *who we are* as human beings and as God's beloved sons.

Throughout life we seem always to be preoccupied by our various "performances"—professional, intellectual, emotional, and, yes, *sexual*. In trying to please those around us, we attempt to appease and accommodate what can sometimes feel like an acute sense of *emptiness* in our own hearts—both, as men and as thinking, breathing, human beings. Yet, apart from all of the actions, acting, and activity of men, we *do* also possess the true capacity to be caring, sensitive, and vital creatures whose capacity and wisdom to love, cherish, honor, and care for others can rival the very women we hope to woo.

It seems that our very process of thinking and living as men has been greatly compromised by early influences from all around us. Subtle instructions to "be like this," or to "be like that," to, "make a lot of money," or to, "be a success," *versus* simply being *who we are,* or becoming *the person we desire to become,* irrespective of financial considerations or the *monetary undercurrents,* may play into our choice of secular goals for what makes "a successful man."

We each strive for success by whatever definition we choose—be it money and wealth, power and influence, or conquest of some other kind. That said, we can easily establish as our *prime directive* the overarching goal of "finishing first with the most stuff," *a.k.a.,* invoking the popular current war-cry, "He who dies with the most toys wins." The fallacy of this temporal (temporary) thought process is precisely the foundational premise of this book: Life is not, and never was, about "finishing first with the most material possessions." Rather, and profoundly, what life *is* about, and what it has *always* been about, is something far more substantial: Life is *eternal,* not *temporal.* Not only do most guys not have the right rule book in their possession, but millions of us are not even playing the real game! *How can we possibly know what the winning goal is?* For that, we must sometimes "take a page out of the book" of the more experienced Christian man.

In a Sunday service a few years ago at Canyon Ridge Christian Church in Las Vegas, Pastor Dick Jorgensen shared a moving message that asked an important question: "How Do I Finish Well?" The essence of Dick's message was that as we become older and wiser, we usually become less concerned with how we finish in temporal ways, yet ever-more interested in whether or not we will *finish well* in the eternal sense. "How Do I Finish Well?" is a question that embraces the ideal that no matter what we have done throughout our lives—no matter how much our lives have been consumed with fleeting things in previous seasons and life-stages—our lives are not over at fifty-years of age, at retirement, nor at any other specified point in time. In God's Eyes, we are valuable at *every moment* of our lifetime, and living well before Him makes a difference for eternity. Though society may no longer see us being "useful contributors," the attitudes, choices, and actions we pursue daily still count for good, bad, or indifferent with God. Pastor Dick's message drove home the reality that while we may retire from our careers, we never retire from doing God's Will. We *can* continue to be vessels of His glory up to our final hour.

Yes, we can merely *finish,* or we can *finish well* living each and every day of our lives to the fullest—*first* for God, and, as will follow, for our own benefit. *Finishing well* is founded on the faith principle that we will one day meet our Lord, hopefully, with a list of accomplishments that reflects a life lived well for Him. Living according to God's Will and doing His will and His work throughout our lives, *all* our lives, is what enables us to finish well in His eyes—having accomplished the work assigned to us. If you're new to all this—to living with purpose so that you can finish well, rather than just *finish out* your life—it's never too late to get started! The race is challenging . . . and the prize? Today: joy, peace, and fulfillment. Eternally: to hear the Master of the Universe say, "Well done, thou good and faithful servant . . . (Matt. 25:21). That is *finishing well!*

Of Faith and Chivalry

Now, let's take this concept of "finishing well" a step further. As a logical outgrowth of finishing well, the incorporation of *chivalrous principles* into our lives as men can have a dual impact on our daily actions. First, it will make us *better* men in the eyes of the women we love, for we will be transforming ourselves from "grunting," insensitive Neanderthals into thinking, thoughtful, sensitive, considerate, perceptive, caring, compassionate, selfless, loving, and emotionally available human beings capable of true intimacy. While that alone would be a desirable goal, add the suggestion that, in setting out to become a *chivalrous* knight, our pursuit of chivalrous ideals and principles will bring us closer to God. This becomes not only a desirable goal for temporal reasons but for spiritual and eternal reasons, as well. If we live as better men, more thinking and more caring, do we not also become *wiser* men, too? If we become wiser men in our thinking and behavior, does not far greater potential exist to find ourselves closer to God? For as *wiser* men (less arrogant, boastful, angry, covetous, grasping, and rude), we will be better able to recognize our own need to seek and find God and to respect and value His Will for our lives.

The pursuit of excellence, then, through the exercise of chivalrous behavior, has two important benefits for a man: It enhances his ability to function as an intelligent, considerate, selfless, loving, and emotionally intimate being, and it improves his ability to live wisely with a greater focus on *eternal* as opposed to the *temporal values.*

Anything else? Certainly! Living by the template for masculine living that embodies the tenets of the "Code of Chivalry" serves to increase a man's appeal to the special lady in his life. In so doing, it greatly improves his potential for a full, rewarding, enriched life as a respected partner in marriage.

By design, the pursuit of honor, dignity, Christian charity, faith in God and His Commandments and principles, coupled with the pursuit of chivalrous living could be seen as important goals in the service of God's eternal Kingdom. Striving for these gives men the hope of and the potential for living fulfilling, happy lives with the women they love—and of staying deeply in love while enjoying true emotional and physical intimacy with them.

Exploring these goals with my fellow men is the hope and objective of this book. In an age of corrupt values and masculine role confusion, I trust that you will find it helpful. May we all find the balance of love and life that I'm convinced men truly seek. To each and every man reading these pages, may God bless you as you do. May this book touch you, reach you, and empower you to become the chivalrous Christian knight that lies dormant within us all.

ACKNOWLEDGMENTS

It would seem most appropriate to dedicate this guidebook on godly chivalry, which I define as "masculine strength with kindness," to four very special and influential women in my life. Through their love, gentleness, interest, inspiration, passion, caring, compassion, support, and fortitude they made an indelible influence on my life and have given me the gift of boundless inspiration.

Four *ladies faire,* you are, individually and collectively, women of timeless beauty, of infinite stature, of magical presence, and of limitless virtue. You represent the epitome of beauty, style, and grace that women everywhere strive to emulate. It is you who have inspired me to commit these musings of a modern-day knight and Christian man to the pages that follow.

First of all, I wish to acknowledge my wife, Judy, the loveliest woman I have ever gazed upon—a woman of timeless beauty and the unquestioned love of my life. Please know that you, dear, most of all, by your love, passion for life, strength, reassurance, and support have inspired me to follow my lifelong dream of becoming a writer. *Thank you, Jude.* I Love You.

Secondly, I give thanks and recognition to Arlene Reich, Judy's mom, who encouraged me to follow my passion for writing by expressing my heart and mind. *Thanks, Arlene.*

Thirdly, to my mom, Eva Jean Oliver Milby, who through her gift of life and her lifetime of love, caring, and sacrifice bestowed upon me the moral values, gentlemanly stature, and the very foundation for living a virtuous life that enabled me to develop into a compassionate Christian man and Southern gentleman and confident soul I now perceive myself to be. Mom, *thank you* for everything. I could not have wished for a more *special* Mother. I Love You.

Finally, to Minnie Milby, my late, paternal grandmother, who went to be with God Almighty in 1988 . . . and who understood me better than anyone ever could. Grandma, I will never, ever forget you.

To these four truly beautiful women of the ages I say, "*You* are true ladies. I love you and I thank you. If indeed I *am* a chivalrous knight, I am all that I am because of your influence and support throughout my life. *Thank You!*

My thanks go also to the Lord God Almighty for His strength, His guidance, and His infinite blessing throughout my life, as well as the gift of divine inspiration to both envision and complete the absolute *labor of love* you now hold in your hands. May these pages reach, touch, and empower many men's souls to seek a deeper understanding of Your chivalry, Lord—of your glory and your well-deserved honor!

Gary D. Milby
January 23, 2006

Chapter One

THE "AGE OF CHIVALRY"

In order to properly understand and appreciate the relevance of the "Code of Chivalry" to the twenty-first century man, it's essential that we examine in some detail the principles that comprised the original Code. One definition of "chivalry" is *the dutiful pursuit of such qualities as bravery, courtesy, honor, and gallantry towards women.* While it was the duty of all medieval knights to be chivalrous, it was expected of all men in that era to adhere to these same honorable principles.

THE ROOTS OF CHIVALRY

The concept of *chivalry* first appeared in Europe in the eighth and ninth centuries (700–800 A.D.). The "Code of Chivalry" was a set of tenets for disciplined and gracious living first designed for the European knights of the Crusades—a series of wars fought by Christians and Muslims between the twelfth and fourteenth centuries (1100–1300 A.D.). The word "chivalry" itself is taken from the French word "*chevalier*," or horseman. The English knight and his French counterpart, the *chevalier*, formed the early beginnings of what would become a major institution throughout Europe for several centuries. The origins of the word "cavalry," or *mounted warriors*, can also be traced to these early knights of the Middle Ages.

"Chivalry" was defined, during medieval times, as *the sworn moral and behavioral code of conduct that governed knights*, whose hallmarks included the embodiment of honor, gallantry, courage, courtesy, generosity, selflessness, loyalty, chastity, respect for, admiration and adoration of women, as well as, other noble traits. During the Middle Ages, Christianity brought together the socioeconomic, political, and military elements of daily life under one cohesive "cultural umbrella" which was used as a unifying element to bring order, civility, and moral definition to the society of the day.

Initially envisioned and implemented as a means of discipline for youthful medieval soldiers readying themselves for battle in distant lands through rigorous daily military training, the concept of *chivalry* evolved into an even larger notion—one that extolled the critical importance not only of being trained *physically* in the art of war with self-discipline, but also, *spiritually*.

Thus, the "Code of Chivalry" embodied integrating overall behavior into an ideal form. It embraced the idea that a knight whose physical, emotional, and spiritual state was at its zenith would result in a totally balanced man and warrior, one whose thoughts, speech, and actions were indicative of the best virtues of manhood one could attain.

Men who distinguished themselves on the battlefield were honored with *Knighthood*.

As the institution of Knighthood grew, more men aspired to acquire the status of being a knight as it offered one of the few, if not the only, means of acquiring noble status without having been born into the noble class. Both the papal Church and national Kings had the power to bestow Knighthood—a highly prized *gift of recognition* of male excellence at the time.

The status of *knight* could be granted in one of two ways: one, the individual could be designated a "Knight Bachelor," or he could be awarded membership in an "Order of Chivalry," an exclusive knightly fraternity. As Kings and the Church began to appreciate the value of chivalry and Knighthood, there was also a recognized need to manage and control the granting of such honors—leading to the formation of "Orders." These Orders were a formal organization of knights and were typically named after a Christian Patron Saint or after a sacred Christian place.

Orders could be *secular;* that is, "sanctioned by a King or Monarch." Or, they could be *faith-based;* that is, "formed by the Church through a high-ranking member of the clergy." Examples of various Orders include: the "Order of the Garter," founded by King Edward III of England in 1348, and the "Order of the Star," founded in 1351 by King John II of France in response to King Edward's Order.

Religion played an essential role in the concept of chivalry. While the Church did not relish the soldier's potential for taking human life, which was the ultimate duty of a knight in battle, the Church *did* recognize the value and utility of a knight to support its doctrines and principles while serving, under God, as its protector. An understanding of *Knighthood* as an institution has, in modern times been transformed into both a *code of conduct* and a *way of living,* and combined with exalted notions of honor, integrity, honesty, and selflessness. While there is much more to the concept of Knighthood in military terms, our focus here will be on the virtuous values of the knight and their relevance to our lives as men today.

THE TEN COMMANDMENTS OF THE "CODE OF CHIVALRY"

Steeped in the very foundations of chivalry is the mandate that in order to be chivalrous, men must exhibit practices of honor, courtesy, truthfulness, and generosity, and it is most relevant in matters associated with courtesy towards the *lady faire.* According to the medieval volume, *Chivalry,* by Leon Gautier, the following tenets form the "Ten Commandments of the Code of Chivalry":

1. Thou Shalt believe all that the Church teaches and shalt observe all its directives.

2. Thou shalt defend The Church.

3. Thou shalt respect all weaknesses and shalt constitute thyself the defender of them.

4. Thou shalt love the country in which thou wast born.

5. Thou shalt not recoil before thine enemy.

6. Thou shalt make war against the infidel without cessation and without mercy.

7. Thou shalt perform scrupulously thy feudal duties, if they be not contrary to the laws of God.

8. Thou shalt never lie and shalt remain faithful to thy pledged word.

9. Thou shalt be generous and give largesse to everyone; and,

10. Thou shalt be everywhere and always the "Champion of the Right and Good against Injustice and Evil."

THE KNIGHTLY VIRTUES

According to early medieval writings, there are *ten* knightly virtues that all men should seek to achieve in daily living:

1. **Prowess**—The knight is to seek excellence in all endeavors expected of a knight, martial or otherwise, seeking strength to be used in the service of justice, rather than in personal promotion or gain.

2. **Justice**—The knight seeks the path of "right," unrestrained by bias or selfish interest. He recognizes that the sword is a weapon of destruction and the taker of human life, so its use must be tempered with the exercise of humanity and mercy. And, if you seek "right," you will earn renown among others.

16

3. **Loyalty**—The knight is known for unwavering commitment to the people and ideals you choose to live by. Loyalty is never to be compromised or taken lightly.

4. **Courage**—The knight knows that choosing the more difficult path is hard, but sometimes necessary, and he is not afraid to choose this path in the pursuit of good and right. He is prepared to make personal sacrifices in the service of his beliefs and the people and country he serves. The true knight also seeks wisdom and takes the side of truth in all matters.

5. **Defense**—The knight is sworn by oath to defend his lord and those who depend upon him. He seeks to defend his lady, family, nation, and all those he deems worthy of loyalty.

6. **Faith**—The knight is faithful in his beliefs, for faith roots him and gives him hope against human despair.

7. **Humility**—The knight first values the contributions of others. The knight does not boast of his own accomplishments, but lets others speak on his behalf. He speaks of others before he speaks of himself, while letting his deeds speak for him.

8. **Largesse**—The knight is generous so far as his resources allow, so that the path of mercy is easier to identify and to follow.

9. **Nobility**—The knight seeks great stature of character by holding to the virtues and duties of his position as a knight. He realizes that, while he may not achieve the perfection of noble ideals, the pursuit of them makes him a better man and knight and brings him closer to God. His nobility also influences others, setting a desirable example in life.

10. **Franchise**—The knight seeks to emulate all that is right, just, and good as sincerely as possible, because it is "right."

The Knightly Virtues outlined above constitute an important template for living and will be referenced throughout this book.

❧THE "CODE OF CHIVALRY"

The "Code of Chivalry" takes the above thoughts and adds additional detail and insight into the daily lives and mandates guiding knightly behavior:

1. Live to serve king and country.

2. Live to defend crown and country and all it holds dear.

3. Live one's life so that it is worthy of respect and honor.

4. Live for freedom, justice, and all that is good.

5. Never attack an unarmed foe.

6. Never use a weapon on an opponent not equal to the attacker's.

7. Never attack from behind.

8. Avoid lying to your fellow man.

9. Avoid cheating.

10. Avoid torture.

11. Obey the law of king, country, and chivalry.

12. Administer justice.

13. Protect the innocent.

14. Exhibit self-control.

15. Show respect to authority.

16. Respect women.

17. Exhibit courage in word and deed.

18. Defend the weak and innocent.

19. Destroy evil in all of its monstrous forms.

20. Crush the monsters that steal our land and rob our people.

21. Fight with honor.

22. Avenge the wronged.

23. Never abandon a friend, ally, or noble cause.

24. Fight for the ideals of king, country, and chivalry.

25. Die with valor.

26. Always keep one's word of honor.

27. Always maintain one's principles.

28. Never betray a confidence or comrade.

29. Avoid deception.

30. Respect life and freedom.

31. Die with honor.

32. Exhibit manners.

33. Be polite and attentive.

34. Be respectful of host, women, and honor.

35. Loyalty to country, king, honor, freedom, and the "Code of Chivalry."

36. Loyalty to one's friends and those who lay their trust in thee.

THE CONCEPT OF COURTLY LOVE

The concept of courtly love blossomed under the patronage of Eleanor of Aquitaine and her daughter, Marie. Its primary theme was the thought that through true love the chivalrous knight would be strengthened by the love of his lady. Couples engaged in a courtly relationship routinely exchanged gifts; further, the lady was wooed by her knight through intricate protocols of social etiquette. She regularly received a variety of "expressions of love"—floral bouquets, "sweet favors," songs, poems, precious stones, and other ceremonial gestures. An interesting point in the art of courtly love was that, in spite of the knight's overt displays of affection and many gifts, his lady needed only return a minor hint of her approval of his "attentions and actions," a mere "Thank you," or other such minor gesture. While she was exalted in word and deed, he made himself her servant, and nothing was required of her in response. This model was exalted as *true* romance, and true *knightly expectation*.

So, while religious chivalry gave the knight his strength through his devotion to God and the Church, chivalry born of courtly love gave the knight additional strength through the love of a woman. This created both the increased desire for and the distanced adoration of women by the knights of the Middle Ages. This love-based chivalry demanded a different set of behaviors, including: courtesy, generosity, monogamy, and the defense of women, while exhibiting the utmost respect for them.

Central to the "Code of Chivalry" are powerful moral and ethical tenets that are essential in defining true virtue: honesty, courtesy, courage, duty to self, duty to one's lady, family and country, loyalty, respect for all (especially women), generosity, fidelity, selflessness, justice, humility, and the pursuit of excellence in all things. These are the foundations of true chivalry, and these values are just as relevant today as they were over a thousand years ago. Chivalry and its principles free a man to speak with his *heart,* as well as, with his mind—elevating him to a new level of being. Respecting this code, he is able to grow both emotionally and spiritually and is capable of true intimacy at multiple levels with the people around him, especially his lady, whom he so desperately desires to touch and love.

Now that we have a sound fundamental understanding of classic chivalry and its monolithic codes, we can move forward and convert the principles of chivalry into terms today's man can use. If we're successful, we will develop the "Codes of Chivalry" listed here into contemporary guideposts for chivalrous behavior among those of us who proudly define ourselves as chivalrous knights, molded and guided by God.

Chapter Two

CHIVALRY IN TODAY'S TERMS

Does the very idea of *chivalry* seem outdated and irrelevant to your life today? *Quite the contrary!* Many, if not all, of the principles of the knightly "Code of Chivalry" are as relevant for men today as they were centuries ago. We've simply forgotten them; or, more alarmingly, we may have misplaced their meaning and import in our own lives. For today's twenty-first century man, with the pressures our society places upon him, it is not only desirable that we aspire to live as those knights who came before us, but it is our duty as men, and more importantly, as godly men, to recover and reestablish the virtues and behaviors so essential to creating quality of life.

It seems to me that all men have the potential of being men of honor. God, in creating man in His likeness, placed that intrinsic possibility deep within the fabric of our souls. We need only to release it to God's glory and to the betterment of our own lives. We need only to allow what we already *know* as right to resume its rightful priority in our hearts, and permit it to serve as a guidepost and a beacon in our everyday lives. Chivalry can help us to do this. *How?*

❧ Are You a Chivalrous Man? (A Short Quiz)

As a first step in this chapter and as we begin the book, this is an opportune time to ask each man reading this book to take an honest assessment of his own life.

Are you a truly chivalrous man?

How do you live your life?

Do you strive to live each day as a man of honor, with gallantry, humility, generosity, love, and compassion while honoring and treasuring your lady and family and following God?

Would you like to rate yourself and find out?

Do you exhibit the characteristics of the knights of some 1,000 years earlier as outlined in the *Code of Chivalry and the Ten Commandments of Chivalry*? If so, which ones, and why do you believe that's the case? Further, in what areas do you feel you fall short of the characteristics of the ideal knight just discussed?

❧ "Chivalry" Quiz!

I'd like to ask each man reading this to complete a short quiz by answering the questions provided below. To the right of each key characteristic of the chivalrous man, please rate yourself, with a "1" being the lowest score you could give yourself, and a "5" being the highest possible rating you could give yourself for that particular attribute and indicative of a very chivalrous man.

RATING SCALE (1 – 5)

(1) LOWEST_____(5) HIGHEST

Please circle the number which best represents your own personal rating with "1" being the lowest rating and "5' being the highest rating.

Part I. The Ten Commandments of the Code of Chivalry:

1. Thou shalt believe all that the church teaches and shalt observe all it's directives	1	2	3	4	5
2. Thou shalt defend the church.	1	2	3	4	5
3. Thou shalt respect all weaknesses and shalt constitute thyself the defender of them.	1	2	3	4	5
4. Thou shalt love the country in which thou wast born.	1	2	3	4	5
5. Thou shalt not recoil before thine enemy.	1	2	3	4	5
6. Thou shalt make war against the infidel without cessation and without mercy.	1	2	3	4	5
7. Thou shalt perform scrupulously thy feudal duties (defined here as your daily responsibilities of family and daily life), if they be not contrary to the laws of God.	1	2	3	4	5
8. Thou shalt never lie and shalt remain faithful to thy pledged word.	1	2	3	4	5
9. Thou shalt be generous and give largesse (giving generously, as much as your resources will allow) to everyone.	1	2	3	4	5
10. Thou shalt be everywhere and always the "champion of the right and good against injustice and evil."	1	2	3	4	5

Part II. The Code of Chivalry:

1. I live to serve my country.	1	2	3	4	5
2. I live to defend my country and all it holds dear.	1	2	3	4	5
3. I live my life so that it is worthy of respect and honor.	1	2	3	4	5
4. I live for freedom, justice, and all that is good.	1	2	3	4	5
5. I never attack an unarmed foe.	1	2	3	4	5
6. I never use a weapon on an opponent not equal to the attacker's.	1	2	3	4	5
7. I never attack from behind (undermine or berate others behind their backs).	1	2	3	4	5
8. I avoid lying to my fellow man.	1	2	3	4	5
9. I avoid cheating.	1	2	3	4	5
10. I avoid torturing (or abusing others).	1	2	3	4	5
11. I obey the laws of my president and country, and the laws of chivalry.	1	2	3	4	5
12. I administer justice (I am just when dealing with others).	1	2	3	4	5
13. I (do my best to) protect the innocent.	1	2	3	4	5
14. I exhibit self-control.	1	2	3	4	5
15. I show respect for authority.	1	2	3	4	5
16. I respect women.	1	2	3	4	5
17. I exhibit courage in word and deed.	1	2	3	4	5
18. I defend the weak and innocent.	1	2	3	4	5
19. I destroy evil in all it's monstrous forms.	1	2	3	4	5
20. I crush the monsters that steal our land and rob (and attempt to injure or kill) our people.	1	2	3	4	5
21. I fight with honor.	1	2	3	4	5
22. I avenge the wronged.	1	2	3	4	5

	1	2	3	4	5
23. I never abandon a friend, ally, or noble cause.	1	2	3	4	5
24. I fight for the ideals of my national leaders, my country, and the Code of Chivalry.	1	2	3	4	5
25. I would die with valor, if need be.	1	2	3	4	5
26. I always keep my word of honor.	1	2	3	4	5
27. I always maintain my principles.	1	2	3	4	5
28. I never betray a confidence or comrade.	1	2	3	4	5
29. I avoid deception.	1	2	3	4	5
30. I respect life and freedom.	1	2	3	4	5
31. I would die with honor, if need be.	1	2	3	4	5
32. I exhibit (good) manners.	1	2	3	4	5
33. I am polite and attentive.	1	2	3	4	5
34. I am respectful of my hosts, women, and of honor.	1	2	3	4	5
35. I am loyal to country and our leader-ship, honor, freedom, and the Code of Chivalry.	1	2	3	4	5
36. I am loyal to my friends and those who lay their trust in me.	1	2	3	4	5

How did you score on the quiz?
How many "4 or 5" ratings did you give yourself which would indicate a chivalrous knight versus how many "1 or 2" ratings did you note, which might suggest room for improvement?

While this quiz is intended as a simple self-assessment (and there is no passing or failing grade) you should now have a better self-perception of where your strengths and weaknesses lie as a potential chivalrous knight.

Your personal results here should prove valuable in your understanding of the principles to follow later on in the book. Now that you've completed this simple quiz, let's move on to a more in-depth discussion of Chivalry in the Twenty-First Century.

❧CHIVALRY IN THE TWENTY-FIRST CENTURY

Chivalry in the twenty-first century is certainly in mortal peril, but it is far from dead. While a majority of men may have little understanding or appreciation of chivalry, there are still many of us, a dying breed of chivalrous knights, perhaps, who occupy seats at the round table and hold firm and fast to the ideals of our fellow knights of a bygone era. While we do not fight our battles from atop our mounts in a field of battle, we do battle every day in striving to succeed in a business world laden with financial, moral, economic, social, sexual, and political pressures and challenges.

Let me say first of all that this book is in no way intended as a means of demeaning men. On the contrary; *as a man,* I am merely attempting to point out the wondrous power and potential we men have at our disposal should we choose to tap into it. While it is indeed true that many men can be Neanderthals in their behaviors and mind-sets—selfish, self-centered, boorish, self-absorbed "jerks" who think predominately with certain of their extremities, far more of us are closet romantics—decent, moral, just men who have the very best of intentions, yet may simply have been sidetracked by misguided notions and the pressures of daily life.

Let me submit to you that the devil, Ol' Satan himself, doesn't want us to be chivalrous, because he loses ground with us, or, more accurately, he loses us entirely to God when that happens. When we become chivalrous, we become *good* (disciplined, honest, respectful, and kind)—leaving a diminished potential for corruption by the evil one, his forces, and his influences. The further away we are from evil, are we not moving ever closer towards God, God's laws, and His grand design? Even so, chivalry and the core-set of behaviors it advocates, can be seen as inherently good for men.

Maybe, too, we men have been somewhat misinformed about *what* and *who* we are and what and who we *should be* by our families, society, our culture, the media, and the evil one, who works through all, innocent in their intent or not. The orientation we all received over the past two to three generations has been consistent with Old Guard guidelines, but with a slightly different twist, gentlemen. It goes something like this: work hard, make money, be a success—accomplishing that success at any cost.

What resulted despite the very best of intentions of our families, in most cases, was indoctrination into values that taught us that our only focus was to be on obtaining "success" in economic terms, with little regard to becoming successful as godly men. In the process of living our lives, some, perhaps many (but not *all*) of us have lost ourselves and our own dreams and goals—possibly while hurting others, including the women in our lives whom we sincerely wanted to nurture and protect—those women who *could* have been in our lives and supported us in living the exciting, spiritually uplifting lives we all dream about and who *may* have become an indispensable part of us if only we had seen the light!

Have you missed the mark with a *faire lady* in this manner? Maybe, if you're honest, you'd have to 'fess up to living some seasons of your life as a decidedly ill-mannered, ungodly man. Not to worry; there's still time to make amends and capture a damsel's heart. Adapting your approach and practicing knightly behaviors may well be the portal to a different and deeply rewarding life for you.

The twenty-first century is and will increasingly become a tough place for all of us. It's even harder to be chivalrous men, let alone, *godly* men, when everything we see and hear around us seems to suggest that to be a chivalrous man is to be a *fool* or a chump. Rather, we're taught by very astute representatives in media and in government—through a myriad of messages—to believe that it's perfectly acceptable, even cool, to be stoic, ruthless, transparent *users* of others, especially women (Have you happened to catch a hip hop or rap video lately?), to be indifferent to women, to use them for what we can get, to take advantage of or to steal from others before they steal from us—with the main emphasis being upon the size of your bankroll. And, we wonder what's wrong with us?

It seems we're being "carpet-bombed," totally and incessantly inundated with the wrong core messages about how to live as men. We see very little around us that would even suggest that a desirable alternative might be to revert back to earlier times to what may just have been a more honorable way of living.

Today's society is a world of being electronically connected, and a world that actually *discourages* interpersonal connectivity or true intimacy. With all of our cell phones, palm pilots, iPods, internet and e-mail connections, we're actually discouraged from intimate, one-on-one communication and contact and sincere, personal communication, which is the only truly *meaningful* communication. While we may talk, we may not be talking about the right things. As well, some men by nature find it difficult to communicate openly in an intimate setting, which places us at even more odds with the lady in our lives because she and her gender embody the essence of interpersonal communication skills.

We men of the twenty-first century should endeavor to understand what it means to be a true knight—sensitive, caring, compassionate, considerate, empathetic, a good listener, emotionally available, and exhibiting a quiet strength. The man who adopts and executes the principles found in the "Code of Chivalry" can become an exception to the rule—a true romantic knight in a world of electronic vassals.

SOME MEN DON'T APPEAR TO HAVE A CLUE OR SIMPLY DON'T CARE

Some men don't understand women, simply don't take the time to try to, *or,* they simply don't care. Even the most accomplished "First Knight" will make a serious blunder, without even trying, at times. Believe me, I know.

For much of the time between my marriages, I admit that I was hurt, confused, and angry—and simply didn't care as much about a woman's feelings or opinions, at least not as deeply as I should have cared. Simply put, I was only interested in myself and in my own immediate gratification, which was certainly a safer position than taking the risk of getting involved and getting hurt again. I am convinced, now, that the major reason for my selfish and non-chivalrous attitude during those years was the absence of God in my life, with limited access to a church-sponsored Divorce Recovery Class or guidance of this nature that might have helped me at the time. I was lost, and thus was fertile fodder for the evil one. And, for a while, I must admit, he had control. But, in time, I began to learn and grow.

I strongly believe that some men have just never learned how to be romantic, feeling, sensitive human beings. First of all, we think that we are not *supposed* to be sensitive or feeling, that it makes us look weak in the eyes of other men and their families, or among the women we hope to impress and about whom we do sincerely care. Secondly, not being well-practiced in expressing emotions, we just don't know *how* to do so.

Take a practical matter: proper table manners. Had it not been for Mrs. Gilpin in senior English class at Southern High School in Louisville, Kentucky, over thirty years ago, I would have no clue about how to hold a knife and fork, nor anything notable about how to behave at mealtime. I'll never forget this: she took an entire hour of class one day and showed all of us how to hold our flatware, where to place it on the table (explaining why), and communicating guidelines on how to eat properly ("Keep your mouth closed. No elbows on the table," etc.). Without her careful instruction in the fine art of table manners, I would have been lost on an important date with a lady and would probably have few good table habits—even today.

The same holds true for many of us; we just don't know what is expected of us by women. So we give up and take the easy way out, or, the *macho*, stoic approach. While this may work for some men, it doesn't work for the vast majority of men or women (as the present U.S. divorce rate will quickly reveal). Still, if we're clueless as men, *how do we get a clue?*

Oh, we could conduct some marketing research, I suppose. As a former marketing research career professional, I can tell you that one of the best ways to gather data is through simple observation of or listening to others. Tell me:

- *Do you observe your lady?*

- *Do you listen to her, I mean, really listen?*

- *Do you truly observe her feelings, her moods, her quiet moments—and appreciate what she says about herself without even saying it?*

- *Have you noticed how she dresses? Or what she might be saying by her manner of dress to us, as men, and to others?*

Just by taking the time to listen to your lady, you can better-determine what she may feel or like from you. Take it from me: the knight who takes time to listen is most likely to keep his *lady faire*.

Men are not generally the greatest listeners, because, we've been too predisposed to talking about ourselves and have a different mind-set altogether about communication than women do. Have you ever been on a first date, and the lady you're with can't stop talking about herself? Weren't you bored to tears? Why would your lady be any different? Do you do the same thing, or are you captivated by her presence, wanting to know everything about her? Listen, listen, *listen,* and learn, learn, *learn.* You may not bat a thousand, but your batting average will certainly improve to major league status.

As for our career life, we may not be "tuned in" to what's really going on there because we've been too preoccupied with the business of becoming a success, as opposed to the business of *being* who we were meant to be. Eventually, a misplaced drive for financial gain can lead to burnout or to the dreaded "midlife crisis." The painful feelings we've been trying to keep down overwhelm us, at last, revealing that we've climbed to the top rung of the wrong ladder! We're a "success," but not where it matters. Don't let this happen to you. Instead, step back; take a minute to answer a few questions in your own mind, and choose your ladder carefully.

Who are you? What are you? What is important to you in your life? Where is your relationship with God? What will be truly important to you in your heart as you draw your last breath? It's a sure bet that you won't be thinking about your 401k or the latest stock quote, but something more like the answer to: *What was my life about, after all? Did I live it well?* These questions and their answers form our core sense of who we are as men, and how our lives will be judged in the way that is meaningful and eternal.

How we're evaluated by God, not by our financial statement, will be the true measure of our life's work and worth. The practice of chivalrous principles in our everyday lives will not only bring us closer to God, guiding us to become godly men, but will mold us into men of better quality, substance, and honor—men with the capability of experiencing true intimacy with the women in our lives that mean so much to us.

❧ THE IMPORTANCE OF CHIVALRY TO WOMEN

Women want to be romanced, elevated, reassured, loved, and cherished. They want a man of class and discretion; a man of polish, finesse, and social grace; and a refined man of taste and conviction. They want and need the constant reassurance that only comes from a true gentleman—a man who is loving, thoughtful, sensitive, caring, generous, considerate, mannerly, mature, and honorable. They also want to be protected and rescued at times.

The man who is a knight *first* and, at the same time, is a good listener has a far better chance at being able to satisfy all of these needs. Women want a strong, yet sensitive and intelligent man, a man who exhibits strength and wisdom while remaining vulnerable and able to share his thoughts and feelings with her. If a man can be both physical, intellectual, emotional, and spiritual and possess all of these traits in sincerity, he is every woman's dream! A man who does not practice chivalrous, knightly principles is highly unlikely to offer his lady such a balance of strengths, because he is not truly enlightened as to his own masculine nature.

We *can* strive to attain to the balance of strength, emotional intelligence, and intellectual intimacy suggested above, but, as with anything good, it will take some time and effort. The adoption of a chivalrous code which can guide our behavior will bring us closer to what we actually desire for ourselves with women, but, are too afraid to admit either to ourselves or to other men—that is, to have an intimate relationship with a woman in which we feel safe and in which we won't be there to exploit or to be exploited ourselves. While men and women are indeed different in many ways, we do share a common bond: we both need and want someone in our lives who loves us, cares for us, and cares about us, and who both respects and admires us.

A true lady loves a chivalrous man. A man who adopts the "Code of Chivalry" in his everyday life is better-equipped to attain the ability to love and cherish another and to be loved himself, also. A chivalrous man has the potential to be regarded as a sexy, desirable, enticing, and alluring man—for a man who thinks, speaks, and lives in this caring and honorable way is a rarity among men. He is strong and decisive, smart yet sensitive—a "finished" diamond, a precious gem that other women have somehow foolishly overlooked. A man with this combination of strength and humble vulnerability is a man who can be reached, who has the potential to be whatever he wishes to be and is a wondrous lifetime companion.

As the chivalrous man makes every attempt to live his life according to God's law and in search of God's truth and his own Salvation, and the man-knight becomes a priceless life-mate. As one in Christ, he and his lady can work together to build a Christ-centered home and work towards their mutual eternal Salvation. And maybe, just *maybe,* men might not be so different from women in the things that matter most . . . if indeed we manifest the values and behaviors of chivalrous knights.

❧CHIVALROUS BEHAVIOR FOR TODAY'S KNIGHT

Adopting a Sir Walter Raleigh mentality, ask yourself these key questions: *Do you open the car door for your lady? Or the door to the restaurant? Do you lay your cape in the road so that she doesn't have to step in the mud? Do you seat her in the restaurant, rising from your chair and extending your hand to help her up as she excuses herself from the table? Why not?* The chivalrous knight would do these things and much more. It's a demonstration of love toward, pride in, and respect for her—and of his *own* pride in being with her, for she is special in his life.

A. Treat Her as the Queen She Is . . .

Do you acknowledge her with bouquets, poems, love letters, and other gifts on no particular date, while always remembering her birthday, your anniversary, and other special dates? Do you hold her hand as you walk together, never walking ahead of her (which demonstrates a lack of respect)? Do you elevate her, making her feel special every minute of the day? Do you continually reinforce your love for her and your undying commitment to your love? A chivalrous knight does all this and much more.

B. Open Doors

Open her doors, any and every door—*always*. It demonstrates knightly respect for her and for yourself, for you are a gentleman, and no gentleman would be caught dead behaving in any other way.

C. Compliment Her

Do you tell your lady that you like her new hairstyle (because you really do)? Do you regularly tell her how pretty she is and how beautiful she looks today? Do you tell her that she smells captivating, even when she isn't wearing perfume? Do you tell her that you like her new outfit? Do you compliment her shoes? Do you tell her that you love her very much and that she means everything to you? Do you tell her that you are proud of her and her hard work, her career, and how well she takes care of you and your children?

The chivalrous knight would do this and much more.

D. How to Seat Your Lady

Seating your lady is a fundamental gesture of the gentleman and knight. When seating your lady, allow her to reach the side of the chair, then pull the chair slowly and gently back about two feet. Allow her to approach the side of the table and ease the chair behind her as she sits. Remain there after she is initially seated, then offer to ease the chair forward as she may need to adjust her seating. Then, you may sit. The knight never seats himself before his lady is seated.

E. Random Acts of Kindness

What can you do around the home to show your lady that you love her? *Take out the garbage?* Move the furniture that she wants put in another room or reconfigured? Buy her a special gift that is unexpected, even a minor thing, is a thoughtful gesture. Even sending her a Hallmark® card or an e-mail—something to reinforce that you love her—can create one of the most precious memories that she will ever have and is the trademark of a true knight.

F. Being Considerate and Loving

Constantly reinforce your love for your lady—from the softest touch and gesture to hugging and embracing her, to your actions of love and caring, both at home, away from home, and in everything you do. The chivalrous man is also a passionate, considerate, thoughtful lover. He places his lady's physical pleasure and satisfaction above his own—for that is what brings him his greatest pleasure. Frequent, nonverbal glances of appreciation, frequent, loving statements of love and affection, as well as what she means to you in your life, all reassure her that she is cherished and secure in your love.

G. Overt Demonstrations of Love

Show her you love her and that you are proud of her in public as well as in private settings—tastefully, of course. Holding hands, kissing appropriately yet with passion and affection, tell her that she is the lady of your life. Overt demonstrations of love may also include arranging for special surprise events, such as a surprise birthday or anniversary party, the giving of a special gift that she has always wanted, or the gift of an unexpected luncheon date with you—the opportunities and methods of expression are endless. The chivalrous knight is both expressive and ingenious!

The chapters that follow provide more thoughts and ideas for the would-be chivalrous knight. The fundamental objective here is to suggest to today's open-minded, moral man a new way of thinking and living. As I've seen in my own and others' lives, embracing the knight's code can empower men to think, speak, and behave in the spirit of those gentlemen of impeccable character who have come and gone before us—men of honor, commitment, duty, courtesy, and selflessness. Their example and their moral code have much to offer modern-day, would-be knights and all who seek to transform their lives through the godly tenets of knightly virtue in daily living while dedicating themselves to the glory of God and to genuinely loving the women He has placed in our lives.

Chapter Three

CHIVALROUS COMPLIMENTS

Do you like it when someone compliments you? *Of course* you do. Everyone does! The chivalrous knight is especially cognizant of this fact. Today's First Knight recognizes the enormous value of paying his lady sincere compliments; further, he relishes every opportunity to do so. Already beautiful without accoutrements, the women in our lives go to a great deal of trouble to look as beautiful and alluring as they do—choosing hairstyles, nail fashions, makeup, clothing, and accessories that communicate artistry and concern for social interaction with others. Sadly, some men simply overlook the obvious. Let's say that again—it's important. *Some potential knights simply overlook the obvious.*

Your lady has gone to a great deal of trouble to look her best for you (and for herself, also; don't kid yourself!) She expects you to notice! *Do you notice?* Further, if you do notice, are you letting her *know* that you notice and that you appreciate her and how nice she looks? If not, you have homework to do, as you do not yet qualify as a chivalrous knight!

❧ARE YOU PAYING ATTENTION?

It absolutely amazes me how little men are tuned in to the efforts women make to look as beautiful as they do. While it's also true that women may dress as much, if not more, for themselves or for each other as they do for the knights in their lives, they *do* make the effort with pleasing results to which we can all attest. Women simply want to be appreciated. So, doesn't it stand to reason that they might like to hear a compliment from you once in a blue moon, if not more often? What do they like to hear? Well, for starters they'd like to hear that you a) noticed something special about them, b) you like how they look, and then, c) you consider yourself fortunate to be beside them.

A very special lady in my life (I'll call her Mary) once told me a story about the time she decided to try a new hairstyle in hopes that her *then* and former husband would like it. After spending hours in the beauty salon and sporting a beautiful new hairstyle that she herself liked, she arrived back home. His greeting was not, "Hi, honey," but simply direct, brutal, and with extreme prejudice.

"I don't like it!" he exclaimed. She was devastated. Little wonder he became the "ex" sometime thereafter.

As chivalrous knights we need to pay attention and be attentive in every way making special note of our lady's daily routine. In observing that routine, today's knight notices how she dresses and what her favorite colors happen to be. He also notes whether she favors a particular outfit or a couple of outfits, and, if possible, learns *why* that is the case. In like manner, what are her favorite pastimes and why? "Too much," you say? "Why do I need to know all that?" you ask.

The answer is very simple: She very likely already knows the answers to these same questions about *you* and is disappointed that you don't know the same about her. Hey, fellas, romance is not *rocket science* but simply a matter of taking the time to care enough to discover what's important to the lady who is so important to you. She *will* notice, and your knightly stature will rise dramatically in her eyes, as well as in her heart.

The challenge for us knights lies in the fact that we may not have been, as a rule, raised to be sensitive, thoughtful, caring, loving, complimentary, and discriminating human beings. Instead, our parents, our friends, environmental influences, and society as a whole may have predisposed us to behave in a somewhat macho, silent, stoic, indifferent, "strong," and ruthless manner—suggesting, for instance, that a "grunt" is the acceptable verbal response to most communications from others. As a result, some of us find ourselves with a decided absence of verbal finesse and social style.

Finesse, in this context, is "the fine art of and ability to recognize an attribute or characteristic that we like, or something that is worthy of compliment or praise in another." *Style* is: "the art and ability to communicate the compliment in a gentle, loving, sincere, yet manly way." Competence in delivering chivalrous compliments using a combination of both *finesse and style* places the knight in the ninety-fifth percentile of all men. These skills should be strived for—even before you address your own wardrobe and social graces, or lack thereof. So, where do *you* place on the finesse scale? Remember, according to the courts and institutions of our land, "ignorance is no excuse for breaking the law."

Do you acknowledge the beauty and allure of her hair? Her new hairstyle? The fact that she just had her hair cut or permed, colored, or highlighted? I have to admit that even as an experienced knight I have missed a few opportunities to show my love and appreciation for my lady here. When you've had a hard day at work and your mind is wrapped up in daily challenges and worries, I know it can be difficult to notice changes in your lady's appearance, and it's easy to overlook such things. It's not that we don't care, so much; rather, it's that men usually haven't been properly trained in such matters. However, if you truly love your lady, it's very much worth your time and attention to comment on the way she's presenting herself to you.

Do you notice her makeup and how nice it looks? How about that new fragrance she's wearing? Do you like it? Have you told her that you like it and that you'd like for her to keep wearing it? She's likely waiting to hear a response to her efforts here, and hearing an unsolicited positive comment from you could go a long way in making her feel very special.

Did you notice the new outfit she's wearing? Did you let her know you noticed, and that you liked it, and mention just why you liked it? Don't merely stop at, "I like it," but tell her *why* you like it. Today's chivalrous knight is eloquent and not only knows how to relay a compliment but is also adept at detailing the reasons for the compliment. If this is difficult for you, you can prepare yourself in advance by forming compliments in your mind that you look forward to giving her soon. With a little effort in this direction, you're now ranked in the ninety-seventh percentile of all men. You do the emotional math!

Oh, let us talk about shoes! The way to most women's hearts is through accessories, and shoes are at the top of the accessories list! Take a tip from Imelda Marcos, the former First Lady of the Philippines who had *thousands* of pairs of shoes. If shoes were so important to Imelda, it would suggest that a lady's shoes must rank pretty high on the fashion scale. If shoes are that important to the lady in your life, just imagine how important they should be to you! In short, are those *new shoes* she's wearing? *Have you complimented her on just how nice they look with her new suit or dress and how well they match her outfit?* OK, how far should you go with this? Well, don't make the mistake of trying to buy shoes *for* her. It's a knightly gesture, but taking her shopping for shoes is an even nicer knightly adventure.

Have you ever just stopped and said, "I just want you to know how nice you look and how beautiful you are today!" And, if you say it, *mean it,* and say it from the heart. Do you have any appreciation for how those words sound to her, or as to what they'll mean to her? Well, if you do, you're now ranked in the top 2 percent of all men.

SHOWING PRIDE IN YOUR RELATIONSHIP

Are you ashamed to be with your lady? *Of course not!* If you were, why would you be with her in the first place? So, if you are proud of your lady and of your relationship with her, why not demonstrate your love, adoration, and pride in the fact that she is an integral part of your life in everything that you say and do?

Remember, women want both to be pursued and admired. Your love, pride, affection, and adoration should show in everything you do on a daily basis. While most men have sent flowers at least *once* in their lifetime, sending flowers on an "anonymous" calendar date, such as a non-holiday, non-birthday, or non-anniversary, etc., is an unexpected demonstration of pure love. This can touch a lady's heart like nothing else, gentlemen. Other key ways of showing pride in your lady and in your relationship are provided below for the knight who cares to listen:

- Listening, with no attempt to provide solutions or to "solve the problem" for her (she may want simply for you to listen, as opposed to your offering sympathy or suggesting solutions).

- Paying the unexpected compliment; privately, and sometimes publicly—for all to hear.

- Having a knightly memory for special dates and landmark historical events in your relationship.

- Reminding her how beautiful she is in your eyes.

- Holding hands, and PDA (public displays of affection).

- Hugs and kisses . . . anytime.

- Treating her as if she's the only woman in the room.

LISTENING

If we fail as men, one of our most glaring failures may be that we don't truly listen to the women in our lives. And, truth be told, we really *don't*, as least not in accordance with our potential to do so. Many women are exceptionally skilled conversationalists, speakers, and listeners. They have learned to survive and thrive through a network of sophisticated contacts and communications—through finessing the gifts of speaking, listening, and intelligence-gathering with a skill that we men can only begin to appreciate, let alone understand.

Women learned long ago the true adage that, "Knowledge is power," in things both large and small, and they are excellent listeners. As good listeners, they miss very little and have uncanny memories, as most men will confirm. Young boys were not raised to be skilled in these areas but were drilled to get a good education, get a job, and to rely upon hard work in order to become "a success." We were simply not indoctrinated by our families or by society at large to become "good listeners." While it's certainly true that we men seem to be well below the grading curve in these areas, when we apply ourselves toward developing good listening skills, it can boost our career success, as well as our ability to respond to a lady's needs and desires, making us a far more desirable knight in their eyes.

So, do you listen, *really* listen, to your lady and what she is saying? Not just what she actually says, but to what she is saying "between the lines?" For example, "Can we have lunch?" may not only mean that she wants to see you, but that she may have something on her mind that she'd like to share with or discuss with you.

When you are together, do you truly listen to her, and can you recall what was said an hour later? The next day? Believe me, your lady can!

Here's a little challenge for every would-be knight that will help you evaluate your present level of chivalry. First, invite your lady to sit down with you for half-an-hour to discuss anything she has had on her mind lately. After you've had an in depth discussion with your lady in private pull out a piece of paper and write down the key points of the conversation.

What did you say? What did you hear *her* say, and what did she talk about? Try to document the facts in as much detail as possible, and then test your own listening skills by bringing up the points you recalled the next time you speak with your lady. Did you remember the details of your last discussion with her, or did you find that she corrected you on one or more details? If you found yourself being "lovingly corrected" on two or more points, chances are that you need to hone your listening skills.

However, whatever you score here, and more and more as your skills improve, your lady will be suitably impressed by the gift you're giving of listening to her and will very likely draw closer to you for it. Welcome to the top 1% of all men, Sir Knight!

❧MAKING NOTE OF DETAILS

Do you observe every detail of your lady's style? How she walks? How she talks? Her favorite words or phrases? How her eyes shine when she looks at you? How she blushes, or how she cocks her head when she laughs or makes a point? The configuration of her smile—or even what prompts her to cry? When you look into her eyes, can you see deep into her soul and tell what she really means or wants to say but cannot?

It is a very good sign for your relationship if you can do this; I assure you! If you can answer *yes* to even a few of these, then, your road to becoming a chivalrous knight is nearing conclusion. You now rank above ninety-nine percent of all males. Welcome to the "Order of the Chivalrous Knight!"

❧PAYING COMPLIMENTS WHEN LEAST EXPECTED

While we touched on this subject a bit earlier, it's important for today's knight to be somewhat unpredictable. I've become convinced that women love a challenge in men and are intrigued and challenged by a man who keeps them guessing, at least a little, and who is somewhat unpredictable in his thinking and behavior. To many women, predictability in men may be synonymous with boredom. If you're no challenge, you're not *interesting*—and thus not worthy of her time. But if you're chivalrous, loving, compassionate, considerate, caring, eloquent, a gentleman knight, and at the same time a bit of a mystery, what a unique combination and a rare catch you are! Besides, why should women have all the fun? Men can be mysterious, too!

Compliments should be sincere and paid often. The knight with good observational and perceptual skills will not find this difficult to do. Don't limit your compliments to the moment when she emerges from the dressing room in an evening gown for that special night out with you (although this is a wonderful opportunity to tell her how beautiful she really is!) Still, at every opportunity—from that simple moment when the two of you are just sitting at home and you notice something about her that excites or moves you, to that moment at a restaurant when the light catches her face *just right,* and she glows in front of you, to a moment when something that's said elicits a response in her that you find particularly enticing and sexy, a praise of your lady's beauty and uniqueness can arise in your mind and flow out from your lips.

Yes, there are an infinite number of opportunities to compliment your lady. But, each time you do so, it must be sincere. Prevarication renders praise ineffective, so *mean it* when you say it—both for your own good, as well as hers. If your compliment and the feelings that prompt it are not sincere, she will know it. Further, paying compliments that you do not truly feel inside will only cheapen the encounter and its meaning for you, also. The experience of paying a sincere compliment, however, should accomplish several objectives:

- It will make a bona fide deposit to her *emotional bank account* (more on this later).

- It will reinforce your sincere feelings of love and affection for her.

- It will reassure her of your love and sincere affection, and;

- It will enhance the level of spiritual intimacy between the two of you and bring you ever closer to Christ's will for your lives.

❧FILLING HER "EMOTIONAL BANK ACCOUNT"

Did you know that you make both *deposits* and *withdrawals* to your lady's "emotional bank account" each and every day? That is, everything we say and do as chivalrous knights is either received or perceived by her as a *debit* or a *credit* in terms of its negative or positive impact on her emotions. You see, gentlemen, when we say or do something positive, or, do something negative which damages or diminishes the relationship, it is, often without official notice to us, "posted" as an increased asset (a positive, a deposit of emotional energy) or a liability (a negative, a withdrawal and a loss of emotional vigor) to your union with your lady. The former is good; the latter, a very bad thing. And, unlike your account at the local bank, a $300 deposit does not have the same emotional value as a $300 withdrawal when dealing with your lady's emotional issues.

For example, and as all men know, we can pay dozens or even hundreds of compliments to our ladies (making *emotional deposits*, in this illustration), all of which are good and energizing to your relationship. But make just *one* negative comment (or "emotional withdrawal") and everything good and positive that you have said or done (built up) for months, or even years, is offset by that one stupid or thoughtless comment. A critical comment about her weight is a great example! It may take us days, weeks, months, years (or it is ever forgiven?) to overcome one comment. We've all been there and, often unintentionally, have been guilty of *overdrawing* our lady's emotional account! Here's how easily that can happen . . . .

❧A SAMPLE EMOTIONAL BANK ACCOUNT EQUATION:

1 (EW) = 50 (ED); or, One Emotional Withdrawal Equals Fifty Emotional Deposits

Your exact equation may vary, of course, depending upon the nature and severity of the withdrawal. Translation: One *bad* comment will offset some fifty (50) positive compliments, so think about what you are about to say and ask yourself the question, "Is saying this an emotional deposit, or will it be a withdrawal?" Again, each knight must do his own math. But as Christian knights, it's important to make *every effort* to make as many "emotional deposits" to our lady's treasure chest as possible, while making every conscious effort to minimize, or, if possible, eliminate emotional withdrawals.

Compliments, thoughtful gestures of love, physical and verbal expressions of your love for her, expressions of thankfulness that she is in your life and communications of the meaning and richness she has brought to your life—all count as emotional deposits. The Bible teaches us that husbands are to love their wives, even as Christ also loved the Church (Ephesians 5:25). It's incumbent upon the chivalrous knight to extol the virtues of his lady and to ensure that her emotional bank account has an ample balance that is at all times maintained "in the black." *Praise elevates the bottom line, gentlemen.* We can further ensure emotional solvency in our relationships through listening and open communication.

HAVING A KNIGHTLY MEMORY FOR DATES AND EVENTS

The lady in your life remembers everything from her sixth birthday party to what you said to her ten years ago, while most men can't remember what we said to our lady over dinner last night, right? Well, today's self-disciplined knight is a virtual fountain of knowledge who can astound and amaze his lady with his knowledge of dates and events, both significant and trivial.

Of course, it goes without saying that you need to keep at arm's reach all key dates and events—the birthday of your lady, as well as that of your in-laws and every other member of her extended family, the birthday of the dog, cat, or other family pet, the day you met, your wedding date, your anniversary, all other anniversaries, and so on. And, if you've got it, *flaunt it!* Let her know that you know, without having to be reminded. Not to do so reduces you to the status of a non-knight, or a *typical male*. Remember, our goal is to distinguish ourselves as knights, far and away different from the stereotype of the "average" male.

How in the world are you going to remember all this? There's an easy solution: buy an appointment book. It's inexpensive, and you can use it for a number of functions. In addition to remembering key dates and events, use it to store other essential information: your lady's clothing sizes (shoes, ring, clothing), key phone numbers, and other knightly key information, including the number of the local florist (where you should maintain an open account), a jeweler, and other support professionals.

REMINDING HER OF HER BEAUTY IN YOUR EYES

Your lady is the most beautiful woman in the world to you, or else you would not have dedicated your life, time, and love to her, right? While the fact that you've done so might be expected to be enough of a testimony so far as men are concerned, it is wholly inadequate in the eyes of our ladies! Today's true lady needs consistent and constant reassurance that we love her, that we are *in love* with her, and that she is the most ravishing, exciting, and inviting creature with whom God has ever graced the face of the earth. It's the mission of every chivalrous Christian knight to remind his lady at every opportunity that she is very beautiful in his eyes and in his world . . . and that she is the one and only woman in that world. (Gentlemen, if your lady is showing signs of emotional strain, it's time to take responsibility for nurturing her according to the biblical mandate in Ephesians 5, not time to "dump" her and start draining somebody else's emotional bank account. Again, check your investment against your return. *Do the math,* and start making deposits—*now.*)

Showing her how much you value her through gifts, flowers, jewelry, and other small treasures is a great idea, and something today's knight should routinely practice. However, *showing* her is one thing; *telling* her is quite another. Be romantic. It's OK. She wants you to be romantic! Telling her of her beauty from your vantage point, how special she is to you, and what she means to you is priceless both in her eyes and in her heart, and is precisely what she wants to hear from you. And, she wants to hear it *often*—not just on your anniversary or on Valentine's Day. Tell her these things often, daily if possible, and as often as you can. Give her all the compliments you can, as often as you can, for as long as you can . . . and watch your lady "rise up on air" before you.

❧PUBLIC DISPLAYS OF AFFECTION, OR PDA

Your knightly pride in the "love of your life" should be immediately apparent in everything you do, including your actions as you walk with your lady. Take hold of her arm, walking hand-in-hand, letting the whole world know that she's with *you,* that you're proud that she's with you, and that you want everyone around you to know it. For all of her positioning, your lady may be insecure about your feelings for her and may desperately need the reassurance that comes from hand-holding and PDA, or *Public Displays of Affection.*

I first heard this term while a college student exposed to the *Upward Bound* Program at Eastern Kentucky University in the early 1970s. PDA refers to "any public expression of affection," such as holding hands, kissing, or other expressions of affection that may, in their exuberance, sometimes exceed the borders of good taste. While I don't advocate "making out" with your lady in public, demonstrations of love and affection, such as holding hands, a gentle embrace or hug, or even a tasteful kiss, indicate that the two of you are happy and in love. Aside from the likelihood of instilling jealousy in everyone around you (which would not be your intention, of course), you will make a statement to the world and to your lady that she is the most important woman in your life (ladies, this works well for you, too!) A public display of affection speaks volumes about the joyfulness and stability of your love for each other and increases emotional security both ways.

PROTECTING HER FROM THE COLD, CRUEL WORLD

The media and the entire planet would have you believe that women are not the least bit interested in being protected from the cold, cruel world. However, I've never subscribed to that theory, and a truly wise, godly man doesn't, either. I suppose I've always been a romantic at heart and have always believed that most, if not *all* women, would love to find a loving, compassionate, responsible, godly man who truly loves them and who is unquestionably in love with them. I've also suspected that many women, while they would never openly admit it, hope and pray for a gentle man who will come into their lives and "rescue them," whether they need *literal* rescuing or not. Because while many women do a wonderful job of taking care of themselves and don't really need a man for financial support, they may wish for a man to be there for emotional support. My feeling is that this human need "works both ways," and is a key part of the plan of God for men and women.

You see, there is a huge difference between seeking *financial* security and seeking *emotional* security, and I wanted to reinforce the distinction. First of all, most women seek a man who is secure enough in himself that he can stand at arm's length and let her be who she needs to be as an individual, yet he is still right there to support her if, and when, needed. While such a balance may be a challenge for a man who is not secure in himself to maintain, it should be an easier task for today's values-driven, chivalrous knight.

THE ART OF BEING CLOSE BY, BUT NOT "HOVERING"

This concept is a very simple one; i.e., today's chivalrous knight develops and perfects the ability to be *close by for support,* should he be needed, yet *not too controlling or overpowering,* so that his lady cannot be the person she is or hopes to become. In other words, the knight is strong and secure enough in himself and in his relationship—and in love enough with her—that he is able to stand clear, allowing his lady to grow and be just who she wants to be. Many men are not yet fully equipped to handle this type of situation, and I am in no way suggesting that it will be *easy* for most men to do, as there exists the potential (through the existence of too much freedom for both parties) for the two to grow apart. Further, taking a stance that allows for too much freedom may suggest indifference on the man's part, which must be resolved. However, with God at the center of the relationship or marriage, the man's strength in being able to "stand by while standing clear" of his lady will only add to the intimacy and quality of his relationship.

❧TREATING HER AS IF SHE'S THE ONLY WOMAN IN THE ROOM!

Treat your lady as if she's the only woman in the room, because if you truly love her, she is! I have seen firsthand and have also heard numerous stories from women I know of men who are out with their ladies but who overtly notice, to the point of ogling, other women.

Nothing could be more insulting! The chivalrous knight wants everyone to know that he is with his lady and that he is proud to be with her. Your total attention should be upon *her,* from your eyes, to your body language, to your chivalrous behavior—opening car doors and other doors, seating your lady, taking her coat and assisting her in putting her coat on, rising both when she leaves the table and upon her return, etc. Treating her with such loving respect is your biblically based responsibility, and it indicates your true affection and respect for God's gift to you—the special lady in your life. Other would-be knights quickly notice your example, your Christian character, your lady's pleasure in you, etc., and follow suit with their own, displaying courtesy and bestowing honor and appreciation on their mate, as is pleasing to God.

Through his own chivalrous actions, today's knight makes his lady the envy of every other woman in the room, and his efforts will be rewarded!

SOCIAL GRACES OF THE CHIVALROUS KNIGHT

To qualify as a *bona fide* chivalrous knight, it's important for today's man to become well-versed in the various social graces. He will need to represent his lady properly, which requires him to behave as a true gentleman. Let's look at some of the social situations that quickly come to mind.

RESTAURANTS

While today's knight need not be a resident expert on etiquette, nor an author of the latest gourmet cooking guide, nor a current subscriber to the *Wine Taster's Almanac,* it's important to have a basic understanding of some common sense guidelines while dining with your lady. Though we cannot cover *all* of the aspects of dining etiquette in this book, we will review basic guidelines on a few key topics.

1. Ordering from a Menu

    When ordering from a menu, there are two schools of thought regarding whether today's knight should order for both he and his lady or, if he should provide her the option of ordering for herself. In my fifty-plus years, I have found that most ladies prefer that the knight offer to order for both, but that she generally prefers to order for herself. This way, the knight has demonstrated the class and discretion of offering to order for both he and his lady while demonstrating his contemporary thinking and maturity by exhibiting flexibility on the subject. "May I order for you? What would you like?" would be an appropriate manner of offering to order for the lady. And, if she asks to order for herself, today's knight is not offended, but graciously acknowledges her desire to enter her own dinner request, and then he does the same.

However, and if wine is desired with dinner, almost every woman will not only desire it, but will expect her knight to take the lead when ordering. Today's knight accepts that there are differences in preferences between women, and he is comfortable in being flexible.

2. What's a Wine List?

    Today's knight must be at least somewhat familiar with a Wine List, if you choose to have wine. Many godly men choose not to drink wine at all; a personal choice. However, a wine list may be politely refused, indicating the knight's preference not to drink. The Wine List provides an inventory of all of the wines, sparkling wines, and champagnes offered either by the glass or the bottle and is listed according to type of wine: white or red, and type of grape: Chardonnay, Merlot, Cabernet Sauvignon, etc. A simple education in wines, either through a short course or by reading a text on wine will more than suffice here. Briefly, most recommend white wine with fish, poultry, and other white meats and with red wine with red meats and various other dishes. Different wines and types of red and white wines go better with certain dishes, and, if ordering wine is your choice, it's perfectly acceptable to ask your waiter for a recommendation.

3. Just Desserts

    Dessert should always be offered. However, since many ladies
    will politely decline the offer of dessert, the knight may take the
    pressure of ordering dessert from her by suggesting that they
    "split" a dessert. That way the lady, who may actually desire a
    bite of dessert, may partake without any guilt that may be as-
    sociated from ordering the additional item. Again, the knight's
    armor becomes a bit brighter.

4. Knightly Table Manners and Silverware

    The mark of a true knightly gentleman is knowing how to
    properly choose and use silverware. Informed use of tableware
    will not only indicate the knight's sophistication and level of
    etiquette, but will compliment his lady. What is essential to
    know here?

    Forks are located to the left of the dinner plate, in order of the
    course being served: first course, salad fork; second course,
    dinner fork, etc. To the right of the plate are located knives
    and spoons, positioned in the same manner. Eating utensils
    are always to be used from the outside in: i.e., outer fork for
    the salad, the next fork for the next item, usually the entrée,
    and so on. Once knives are used, they are never to be placed
    back on the table, but should be placed at the perimeter of the
    dinner plate, blade-side in. Today's knight demonstrates his
    knowledge of table etiquette, thereby complimenting his lady's
    gentility. For more information on table etiquette, consult the
    Internet or your local library.

AUTO ETIQUETTE

1. Opening Doors

    Always open the car door for the lady in your life. It demon-
    strates your genuine respect for her, and makes the statement
    that you are a true chivalrous knight.

2. Valet and Tipping

This is something that I know a great deal about—having worked my way through high school, college, and into my first home by parking cars as an auto valet. Today's knight immediately obtains the respect of the valet by calling him or her by name upon exiting the car (very few knights do *this*, and it will immediately set you apart). Ask to be kept "up front" while providing an immediate tip (two or three dollars is usually adequate) to the valet. Your "advance" tip states that you want and expect good service, are used to receiving it, and are willing to pay for it. If you don't want good service, don't offer an up-front tip. You'll be treated like everyone else! Up-front tipping knights do not take such chances.

Upon your departure (unless it's a large Las Vegas casino), they will know you by sight and will likely already have the car up front (like your tip), and you're on your way. No waiting, and your lady doesn't get cold in the winter air. Today's knight offers a good "exit" tip (three to five dollars, or more, depending upon your venue), especially, if a second valet offers to open and close the door for your lady! Good service demands an equally good reward and says a great deal about the knight's taste and style, both to others and to your lady! However, do *not* tip for poor service! Today's knight also uses discretion on this matter, as well.

3. Coats and Wraps

It should be "second nature" for the chivalrous knight to always help his lady on and off with her coat or wrap—with no exceptions. When a coat check is available, offer to check the coat, unless your lady would prefer to keep her coat beside her. Either is fine, but do offer. Be sure to tip the coat check staff, as well.

4. Social Functions

Today's knight handles himself with grace and style at all social functions. The knight should be attentive—first to his lady, ensuring that she is comfortable and that she has food or a refreshment, if she so desires. Introductions should be of the lady first, and then of the knight, unless the lady is making introductions. The same mannerly actions that apply elsewhere also apply at social functions: seating the lady, opening her car doors, etc. As in other situations, the knight shows his pride and pleasure in appearing with his lady, demonstrating his gentlemanly attitude and demeanor to all present.

Family and Friends

Whether you're with *your* family or with *her* family, the knight must carry himself with class, manners, and with the utmost discretion. While it's not only acceptable but desirable to show pride and pleasure in being with your lady, overt public displays of affection should be avoided. Common sense in behavior goes a long way in guiding the knight among family and friends. Of course, all of the social graces discussed earlier should be followed here, as well.

Remember that you're with *her* only, and, as stated earlier, always remember that the chivalrous knight shows his lady his undivided attention and makes her "the envy of every other woman in the room" through his attentiveness, his tasteful demonstrations of affection, and his discretion. He sees to her absolute comfort and every need, while staying at arm's length, permitting her to enjoy the setting and the other guests present.

A True Knight Is a Godly Man

First and foremost, today's knight is a godly man, and he follows the Word of God and the teachings of Jesus Christ, the Son of God, not only in church but in his everyday activities, in his interactions with others, and in the affairs of love. The godly man also believes that Jesus Christ is the Son of God, and has professed Him as his personal Lord and Savior before men. Further, the godly man has been baptized through immersion, rising from the cleansing waters in newness of life and attitude.

The character of the godly man is in no place more evident than when he is in the presence of his lady. Reflecting the virtuous goals of Christian manhood, the Ten Commandments of the "Code of Chivalry" were a recruiting theme employed throughout the history of knighthood and were based in large part on showing respect toward the Church. In fact, three of the Ten Commandments of the "Code of Chivalry" specifically reference God and Church, and thereby set the very tone for today's Christian Man:

- "Thou shalt believe all that the Church teaches, and thou shalt observe all its directions."

- "Thou shalt defend the Church."

- "Thou shalt perform scrupulously thy . . . duties, if they be not contrary to the laws of God."

Chivalrous behavior is, then, the execution of the earliest Christian principles of *prowess* (the search for excellence in all endeavors), *justice* (seeking the path of right), *loyalty* (unwavering commitment to the people and ideals you choose), *defense* (of your family, of your nation, and of those worthy of loyalty); *courage* (the willingness to make personal sacrifices for what is right), *faith* (faith in one's beliefs, which gives hope); *humility* (value of others' contributions first); *largess* (generosity, as resources allow); *nobility* (a noble character, which grows in stature by looking upward, towards heaven); and *franchise* (copying and attempting to emulate all that is good, with all sincerity).

Not there yet? That's OK; simply by striving to reach these chivalrous goals, your character grows in nobility and increases in favor with God, mankind, and womankind. This will, in time, return rich dividends in your life and in the lives of those you care about. Now, let's take a look in the mirror.

Chapter Five

THE WELL-DRESSED KNIGHT

The chivalrous knight is a well-dressed man. What does dress mean to her? Grooming communicates a respectful attitude—towards yourself and towards others. If a man does not show respect for himself by dressing well, why would she choose to be with him? As a knight, would you choose to be with your lady if she dressed in a careless manner that rendered her physically unattractive? *There you have it.*

Your lady wants to be proud of her knight and wants to know that other women find him both attractive and desirable. A well-dressed knight is an attractive and sexy knight, a gentleman worthy of the company of a lady.

How the chivalrous knight dresses—how well he dresses and his attention to detail in his manner of dress—says a great deal about his opinion of himself. If your manner of dress suggests that you are unsophisticated, are indifferent about the way you dress, and care little about your appearance, your lady is highly unlikely to respect you, or be interested in being with you for long. Why?

Because how you look is a snapshot of who you truly are, revealing your priorities, your ambition, your self-image, your educational level, your affluence and maturity, your self-esteem, and your desire for success. In short, your level of attention as to how you dress is a reflection of the knight that you are—or *are not*. Today's lady wants to be with a man who is not only successful but who takes pride in his own appearance, for *himself* first, as much as for her or for anyone else. Being well-dressed says the following about you:

- You have high self-esteem and know that you have an influence on others.

- You are successful and success-oriented.

- You are well-educated (formally or otherwise).

- You are ambitious—and want to practice your skillfulness among others.

- You exude sex appeal and attract others to yourself.

- Your personal appearance (and good hygiene) are high priorities.

- You are prosperous, comfortable with yourself, and others.

- You possess attention to detail; you care.

- You respect yourself, and you respect those who will share their company with you.

THE DEFINITION OF "WELL-DRESSED"

The term "well-dressed" means different things to different people. To the chivalrous knight, it means caring enough about your appearance to seek the help of clothiers, tailors, and other fashion consultants in order to assist you in creating the desired image that you, as a knight, wish to communicate. Generally, however, a well-dressed man may be defined as a man who tastefully coordinates his clothing items in respect to color, style, current fashion, and as a *reflection of the man* himself.

Suits should be of proper fit and well-tailored to the man, with shoes, socks, belt, and other accessories being of matching color and texture. Neckties should complement the suit, not conflict with or overcome it. Colors of clothing should complement the knight's skin tone, while the style of clothing should complement the knight's height, weight, and body style.

Well-dressed also means well-coifed, with hair and beard neatly trimmed.

FROM JEANS TO BLACK TIE

Today's chivalrous knight is a man for the twenty-first century, and he is as comfortable in formal attire as he is in jeans or casual wear. If the man is not totally comfortable in various types of dress, perhaps now is a good time to experiment with a new look or to get comfortable with a different type of clothing than he normally wears, such as changing out blue jeans and a T-shirt for dress casual slacks and a button-down shirt. For instance, what have you *not* tried in these three categories?

1. Casual Wear

    a. Dress slacks, properly cleaned and pressed.

    b. Casual, polo, or dress shirts (dry-cleaned and/or pressed).

    c. Casual loafers or shoes (shined).

    d. Casual socks (subtle pattern to match, darker than slacks).

    e. Casual belt (matched to the color and tone of the shoes).

    f. Hair (neatly groomed).

2. Dress Wear

    a. Suit (properly cleaned and pressed).

    b. Dress shirt (cleaned and pressed).

    c. Dress shoes and socks (with color and tone matched to suit color: black/black, brown/brown, etc.).

    d. Dress belt (matched to color and tone of shoes).

    e. Dress socks (subtle pattern to match, darker than dress pants).

    f. Hair (neatly groomed).

3. Formal Wear (Black Tie):

    a. Tuxedo (black or, as specifically advised for function).

    b. Shirt (select to match tuxedo and to personal taste).

    c. Tie (black; or color-matched tie and cummerbund; or white tie).

    d. Cummerbund (optional; if worn, black, no colors).

    e. Shoes (formal, black).

    f. Hair (neatly groomed and cut within past three to five days)

To many, being well-dressed is a matter of personal tastes and preferences. While I in no way mean to suggest what is precisely right for *you*, today's knight is encouraged to seek the advice of skilled clothing store consultants and tailors when appropriate in order to arrive at the best look. If you and your lady have a sound relationship, it is acceptable to ask for her opinion regarding fashion decisions. In fact, relying upon her input and fashion sense will ensure that she approves of your method of dress.

Jeans are fine, given the appropriate setting. However, today's knight does not limit his wardrobe to wearing only blue jeans (which makes him pretty predictable; i.e., *boring),* but exhibits a wide range of looks, from very casual to formal. A wise man's wardrobe reinforces the man's wide range in interests and tastes, making him more interesting and desirable to his lady.

MATCHING YOUR CLOTHING TO THE OCCASION

Just as knights of old dressed in armor or in velvet to meet their dragons and/or *ladies faire*, matching one's clothing to the occasion is mainly a matter of common sense. Just so, the well-dressed, twenty-first century knight matches his suiting to the particular occasion. For an event that you and your lady will attend together, feel free to ask her what she plans to wear—if she doesn't ask you first. If you need help matching your clothing choices for a particular family or formal occasion, I have found the staff of *Men's Wearhouse* stores to be an excellent, helpful source of wardrobe advice; their stores are a wonderful source of quality men's fashions. Department stores like *Dillards, Macys, Nordstrom, Neiman Marcus,* and *J.C. Penney* can also be excellent sources of fashion assistance for men. If fashion is not your forte, not to worry! It is for *some* men and women, and they're usually more than happy to help you dress for success when asked to do so. Ask. "You're gonna love how you look, sir."

Chapter Six

THE WELL-READ, WELL-TRAVELED KNIGHT

It is ever-more critical for the chivalrous knight to be well-read and well-traveled, particularly in light of current events that demand our awareness of the preciousness and frailty of life. The violent, sudden, and tragic September 11, 2001, terrorist attacks on the Twin Towers of the World Trade Center in New York, the Pentagon in Washington, D.C., and the plane crash in the Pennsylvania countryside all during the same day illustrate the fact that rapid-fire change is occurring in our world, requiring both adjustment in our way of living and a soul-searching reassessment of the priorities we've established for ourselves as a nation.

The chivalrous knight is all-too aware of these and other areas of social upheaval around him. He values information as a means of making informed decisions on strategy and "course correction" for himself and his lady as they travel life's course together. Going a step further, events such as 9-11 bring into sharp focus the critical importance of being knowledgeable on world events and of local happenings around us, all the while maintaining an appreciation for the preciousness and fleeting nature of life and living every moment to the fullest.

The events of 9-11 force us to examine the current direction and meaning of our lives and prompt us to ponder our future after death. While the three-thousand-plus souls who perished that day had no warning that this was to be their last here on earth, their sudden passing has granted all who remain an opportunity we may not have had before—a chance to reexamine our lives and make changes, where necessary, while we still can.

Life is meant for living. Why don't more of us live our lives more fully? I've never understood that. Maybe the terrorist attacks of September 11, 2001, in spite of all their horror, remind us all of something very important. Life is fleeting—are you living the life you want to live? Far more significantly, are you living a good, decent, Christian life? If not, what do you intend to do about it?

To be *Epicurean* is to follow the old Roman motto: "Eat, drink, and be merry, for tomorrow ye may die!" Women have always seemed to grasp this pursuit of fulfilling experiences far more than men, possibly because women seem to be far more aware of the passage of time and of life's stages than do men. Whether due to an internal, ticking clock or simply as a reflection of what Mom taught her as a young girl, women simply seem to live their lives at a more accelerated, Epicurean pace than we men do, and they fill it as jam-packed with activity as possible, without apology. Conversely, many men simply seem to take a "sitting under the shade tree having a lemonade-type" of attitude in living their daily lives, and thus miss many opportunities to grow and truly experience life.

It's been said that 98 percent of us are asleep with only 2 percent of us actually being "awake." I believe it. Look around you. Who can you point to, especially a male, who actually lives every moment of his life as if it were his last—with elegance, active compassion, Christian charity, grace, honor to others, and love? That man is a true knight, and the desire of every woman. Why? Because he *gets it.* He understands. When you see the vast majority of us who drone through our daily existence without ever really living, it does appear true, indeed, that very few of us ever realize that our time is short; that life is meant to be lived—and lived fully.

The chivalrous Christian knight's focus is on the *eternal,* versus the *secular* and temporary nature of our existence here. Consequently, he is secure in the knowledge that he is forgiven and saved through grace by his belief and trust in Jesus Christ and that he has eternal life. Knowing that he is saved through grace, he is naturally "tuned in" by his very focus on heaven and eternity, enabling him to enjoy the truly valuable aspects of life here on earth, while remaining ever-vigilant about matters concerning heaven and the world to come.

Now, here's where the well-read and well-traveled knight comes into play. "Ah, (as Shakespeare said), the play's the thing . . .!"

THE WELL-TRAVELED KNIGHT

The chivalrous knight of the twenty-first century will be the man that is well-read and well-traveled. He will at least be familiar with current events, the latest political and social issues, and issues that affect his and his lady's life. He will have at least a rudimentary knowledge of the most popular authors and will be a daily reader (or at least a serious scanner) of his daily city newspaper and/or *The New York Times, The Washington Post, The Los Angeles Times, The Chicago Tribune,* or many other leading dailies around the country. He will be a man who appreciates the arts and humanities and a man who willingly accompanies his *lady faire* to the opera, the philharmonic, the theater, special theatrical events, Shakespeare festivals, the latest art exhibit on the post impressionist masters, a book signing of her favorite writer, or other activity of import to his lady. And the true knight will not only attend such events but will initiate plans and finalize the arrangements for many. He will demonstrate a manly Christian balance of culture, breeding, and character—whether he hails from the city or from the most rural corner of the kingdom.

Where we came from in terms of upbringing in youth is in no way an indicator or barrier to where we can go as a chivalrous knight if we desire to grow in our knowledge and understanding of the wide world around us.

Most ladies do not want a knight who defines an evening as two people watching television while he sits on the sofa eating snacks and drinking his favorite beverage. Those vassals are a dime a dozen. What is truly a rare find is a knight who is not only well-dressed and handsome but a man who knows his world and is aware of the people and events around him. The *conveyance of awareness* is one of the sexiest attributes the knight can exhibit to his lady. *Awareness* in this context can best be defined as a man's understanding of the places and events surrounding him, concurrent with his ability to deal with and manage these events, while serving as both facilitator and protector for his lady.

In short, the well-read and well-traveled knight's knowledge, culture, and awareness of current culture in his world and his ability to grasp and successfully take advantage of this makes him an exceptional find, an attractive prize, and extremely sexy. Men well-schooled in the arts and literature are hard to find, and a godly, self-educated knight who is also a loving man of compassion and who adores his lady is almost an impossible dream. Most women likely gave up on the idea of finding such a mystical combination of strength and kindness in a man years ago. Imagine the excitement when you appear!

The point is this: *you* can be that rare find! How will you prepare yourself today?

Being Well-Read Makes You Sexy

What books and authors have you read in the past six months? Do you read the Bible daily, or at least regularly? Are you part of a Men's Bible Study group? Are you a daily reader of the local newspaper . . . and not just of the comics? Have you ever heard of D. H. Lawrence or John Steinbeck? Have you read any of their works?

Being well-read expands your knowledge of the world and frees you to grow and experience more of what life has to offer. It also makes you more sophisticated and better able to converse on a myriad of topics in a variety of social and intimate settings.

❧THE "WELL-READ TEST"

Here's an exercise to assess whether you are well-read. Make a list of all of the books you have read in the past a) month, b) year, c) two years, and, d) five years. Have you read at least two full-length books during the past six months? Five books during the past year? What were they? Were they scholarly books dealing with serious social and political issues, or were they lighter treatments, or books on sports or similar activities? More importantly, what did you gain by reading the book? What did you learn from reading the book that has helped you in living an "improved" daily life? We may read a lot, but what we may not be doing is reading books that help us to live fuller lives.

Make your list, and, then, honestly and impartially, note to the right of each work what you learned from each book that has actually helped you to live a better and richer life. If at least some of the books you are reading are not helping to enhance your life experience, think about your book selection. If your list is too short, think about establishing a goal of reading at least one book a month or every other month. Reading only one book a month will add up to some 300 books read over a twenty-five-year time span. Imagine how much more knowledge you will have gained by reading these! And, as a knight, imagine the increased knowledge you will have gained about others and what is going on around you!

Being well-read is another way of expressing your life in a noble *give-and-take* with others that rejoices in the knowledge that it has not been wasted but has been well-lived . . . .

❧AN EDUCATED MAN IS A TURN ON!

No woman worth her salt would waste five minutes with an uneducated, ill-mannered, ignorant knight; wouldn't you agree? Turn it around. Would you like to spend time with a lady who doesn't have something meaningful to say? Most intelligent, chivalrous men would say, "Definitely not." So, if you do little or nothing to educate yourself or to increase your understanding of the world around you, would you want to be with yourself? *Probably not. And* if you wouldn't, why should she? A knight who speaks eloquently and who exhibits a sound command of the language (being fluent in English is a decided *plus,* but fluency in several languages is even better!) is a qualified man who is prepared to represent his lady and care for her. While your lady is certainly capable of "taking care" of herself, she chooses to allow you to "care for her," because she believes that you add interest and enjoyment to the mix.

A well-educated man is far better prepared to "care for" his lady, as he is a far better communicator and reflection of her own good taste, ambition, and desire for success and in living life to its fullest. Cyndi Lauper said it so well in the title of her 1980's hit song: "Girls Just Wanna have Fun." It's true. They do. But, an educated man makes her fun even "more fun," as she can be proud of her special knight who is not only handsome but well-educated and smart. Smart is sexy, too. Very sexy, indeed. An educated man thinks "above the waist," and, again, those vassals that think "below the waist" are too numerous to count. On the other hand, men who think "above the waist" are a rare commodity.

Would you rather be one of many, or a rare commodity? Tough choice, for you and for her! If you're a college graduate, congratulations. Have you thought about graduate school—or at least about taking additional courses in a new field of study? If you have not started your degree, *why not?* If you've started on your degree but have been unable to finish, why not finish? I taught part-time at the college level for over twenty-seven years, and I can tell you that the experience dramatically increased my knowledge, not only in the classroom, but of life itself. Education is not merely a four-year or a six-year college experience, but a *lifetime* experience. We should be learning new things all our lives. To stop learning suggests that you've stopped living. Have you stopped learning? If so, it's time to get back to the business of education and living.

KNOWING YOUR WAY AROUND A WORLD ATLAS

Do you know where the United Arab Emirates is located? How about Yemen? Antigua? Madagascar? Knowing your way around an atlas is another means of expressing the quality of a knight's education, or lack thereof.

Today's knight cannot be capable of conducting an intelligent conversation without a fundamental understanding of the world's geography and where these subject countries are located. Know where the hot spots of the world are located physically on the map, as the "where" may well add to your understanding as to "why" something may be occurring. Simple geography can many times be an indicator of historical or physical meaning. The knowledge-able knight not only knows what is happening, but *where,* and most likely, *why* it is happening. He can point out the location on a map.

Keeping Up with Current Events

Again, ignorance is not bliss. Not being aware of the world and what's happening around you only detracts from your stature as knight of your castle. The reading of your daily newspaper should be a routine practice, even if you only have enough time to scan the key articles. Many knights supplement their information on current events by watching some of the better news outlets: CNN, NBC, and MSNBC are among my favorites for good, reliable news and information. The internet is also an excellent means of obtaining news 24/7. Also, there are a variety of good sites, including the news channels mentioned above, which also maintain excellent web sites. Maintaining a good knowledge of current events, both locally, nationally, and internationally only adds to your appeal as a knowledgeable knight. Further, it should be the *mission* of every Christian knight to keep a vigil on current events. You must be aware of the great enemy, Satan, in order to combat him. Knowl-edge is power, especially against the forces of evil.

Trips and Traveling with Your Lady

When planning a trip with your lady, the prudent knight com-pletes his planning ahead of time and gathers information on the destination and the best routes, including airline routes, schedules, and fares, and at the most economical cost. A lady will appreciate the knight who takes the initiative in making copious plans for ensuring a pleasurable trip.

When traveling, the knight sees the comfort of his lady as the very highest priority. Does she have what she needs in clothing, accessories, toiletries, medications, and other items? Have you made the necessary arrangements and confirmed the same with airlines, hotels, transfers, sightseeing tours, auto rental agencies, and special activities in advance? The knight's duty is to see that his lady's comfort is not compromised in any way.

Chapter Seven

FOREPLAY IS "24/7"

❧FOREPLAY IS EVERYTHING YOU SAY AND DO, EVERYDAY

The term *foreplay* is typically associated with the intimate activity that takes place between two lovers just prior to the act of making love. There's an old joke that for some men foreplay can be defined as the time it takes him to take off his clothes or the thirty seconds of physical touch that occurs just prior to the act of lovemaking. Some men may well have missed out on not only the meaning of good foreplay in a sexual sense, but the value of "foreplay as a concept of living." Experience shows that both are vitally important to the success of a relationship.

Women and men are quite different sexually, as we all know. However, some men either don't appreciate the full range of meaning in the term *foreplay,* or they simply aren't all that concerned with "going for the gold" in their sexual relationship. While almost every man can be ready for sex in world-record-time (1.6 seconds is the current record, I believe . . . just kidding), women both need and want good foreplay, not just to be physically and emotionally

71

ready to enjoy a better sexual experience but also for their own enhanced pleasure and emotional bonding.

Nevertheless, some men tend to overlook the fact that the absence of good sexual foreplay prior to intimacy only minimizes or eliminates the chance that his lady will achieve her maximum pleasure potential. As genders, we're just *made* differently, and the differences must be recognized and appreciated if we are to become good knight/lovers.

The purpose of this book is not to present a discussion on sexual technique but to identify the keys to a *quality of life* for today's knight. It's obvious to this author as a man and educator, that the most effective way of conveying some key points is to begin with the sexual example. *Agreed,* ladies? We'll leave the clinical discussion of sex to the "experts," however.

❧ WHAT IS FOREPLAY, REALLY?

Many a vassal has assumed (and mistakenly so) that foreplay consists of the skill of briefly stimulating his lady in a physical, sexual way immediately before intercourse. Foreplay, in an intimate setting, and shared patiently and lovingly between marriage partners as part of the act of lovemaking, certainly elevates the experience. To the skilled knight, foreplay is far more than a sexual concept. In fact, foreplay, when properly understood and incorporated as an integral art in the daily life of a chivalrous knight, becomes an essential component of all that he does.

Foreplay can be defined as "each and every activity, gesture, or comment from the chivalrous knight to his lady, each and every day." Thus, as the saying goes, "foreplay is a 24/7 proposition." Dedicating attention to it has the potential of greatly enhancing the quality of the relationship between two people, and today's chivalrous knight sharpens his artfulness by engaging in foreplay daily.

Foreplay is not a "five minute proposition." The chivalrous knight realizes that his lady is not the least bit interested in a man that "comes and goes in a heated rush," as a popular Pointer Sisters song puts it. A man in that kind of a hurry is not truly committed to his lady—and she knows it. The wise knight both understands and appreciates his lady and her wish to preserve this moment of intimacy. He wishes as much as she does to prolong it as a lasting memory. Simply put, your lady wants to maximize her own pleasure, just as you do, and this is only possible with a patient, understanding lover. Are you a "five minute proposition?" None of us wants to think that we are, but are we? Our love knows, as do we. *What's the difference?*

Foreplay is not about the five minutes it takes a man to remove his clothes before sex, but about everything he has done during the last day, week, month, year, or many years to prepare for the moment by reinforcing his love for his lady. On a personal level, this includes *what* you have said to your lady and the loving way in which you've said it, the expressions of caring concern you have demonstrated to her, to her family, and to her friends. It involves saying, "I love you" through flowers, special dinners, and time spent together in which you've reinforced your love for her. All of these caring acts are part of true foreplay.

Inconvenient, you say? *What's the payoff*, you ask? If you've heard nothing else here, gentlemen, I can tell you, again, that when there's *no investment*, there is also *no return*. The relationship between 24/7 foreplay and your lady's "emotional bank account" cannot be overestimated.

THE GREAT LOVER LOVES GREATLY

Sex, like most anything else, gets better with lots of practice. I would suspect that almost any man has the potential to become a good "mechanical and technical" lover if he simply engages in a lot of sex. However, I strongly believe that it takes a man of loving patience, caring, and understanding to become a truly loving man in an intimate setting. If foreplay has been a 24/7 priority, the loving, chivalrous man has created an environment that is especially fulfilling and exciting for his lady, which almost certainly will make the sexual experience an emotional as well as a physical one. Which do you think she'll remember as being more truly special?

If you have an active sex life, it's likely that your mechanical skills are very good and that you may be perceived to be a "good lover." But a good lover is a long way from a man who is truly in love with a woman. The difference in the quality and intensity of his lovemaking is unmistakable. The man who is in love with his lady demonstrates an ongoing love affair surrounded by patience, love, and an accommodating presence that the merely technical lover cannot even comprehend.

The married couple with a good, active sex life will know or should know each other's intimate needs and desires, and with both frequency and quality of intimacy, their lives together can become extremely fulfilling. Being merely a good lover "mechanically" and not a good lover "emotionally" is never the true goal of a good knight.

Great sex is wonderful, but it's no match for the expression of unrequited love. *What does that mean?* Let me explain. All women long for a man who has both the ability and the uninhibited nature to express his most intimate feelings—not only his feelings of love for her, but also of his hopes, dreams, feelings, fears, and observations about life. Practice opening up to your lady in this way and you will see a response like no other as she perceives that you trust her and are emotionally open towards her. "Like begets like," gentlemen. Try it and see!

Foreplay also includes the verbal expression of love for your lady. As a good knight, you should tell her often, and in many different and unpredictable ways, that she is the only one for you. Your expressions of knightly love should be diverse, both in public and in private, and they will serve as a constant reinforcement of your sincere love for her.

SINCERE EXPRESSIONS OF UNREQUITED LOVE

- Tell her that you love her—often and in many settings, both public and private.

- Tell her *why* you love her: i.e., as Elizabeth Barrett Browning put it: "Let me count the ways . . ."

- Tell her the moment that you first fell in love with her and what made it happen for you.

- Tell her that she will always be first in your life, and mean it when you say it.

- Tell her that you are proud of her and that you appreciate her and all that she does for you and for others in your lives.

- Tell her that she is the most important person in the world to you, and prove it by your words and actions every day of your life.

- Make God and your faith in Him and in His Son Jesus Christ the center of your marriage with her, and tell her *why* God is at the center: because you care about her soul, and that you love her so much that you want to be there with her in eternal paradise.

- Demonstrate your love for her with unannounced flowers and gifts.

- Demonstrate your love in the simple things you do together.

- Demonstrate your love by sending a simple note, text message, or e-mail: "I love you."

- Demonstrate your love by calling and just saying, "I love you" every day of your life, if possible.

- Demonstrate your love by remembering every date, birthday, anniversary possible (you can write it down in a little black book; they have other uses, you know.)

- Demonstrate your love for her by being a patient, compassionate, attentive lover.

- Demonstrate your selfless love by being a "good listener."

- Demonstrate your love by caring for her both emotionally and financially.

- Demonstrate your love by being there for her, whenever she needs you.

Selfless love is love that asks for nothing in return, and yet always desires more connection with the beloved. It is pure, unconditional love and love that gives of itself with boundless energy. If you are able to position your love toward your lady in this manner, it will make your love rare and profoundly intimate—going far beyond the capabilities of a merely sexual intimacy. And, it will stand the test of time. I know this firsthand.

Finally, your expressions of selfless love will add to your knightly stature and make you a most desirable *bed* and *life-mate* for your lady.

Foreplay Is Taking Time to Know What She Needs: Physically, Sexually, and Emotionally

Listen to the sounds of your lady. What is she saying, both out loud and silently, "between the lines?" What is she telling you she needs, and what is she actually *suggesting* that she needs but is not verbalizing? As a man, it has perplexed me greatly, but I have observed that many women may feel insecure about actually *saying* out loud what they need. Yet they still expect us to somehow figure out what they actually need. Our ability to do so makes us better men in their eyes. As knights we can learn a great deal by taking time to listen both to what is being said and what is *not* being said. Make no mistake, knights: women hear absolutely everything you say, and every single word is an entire novella to your lady—one that is thoroughly processed and analyzed for deeper meanings—so take great care in each word you utter and be sure that it does not injure, wound, or upset her (remember, one withdrawal from her *emotional bank account* offsets some fifty or more deposits which have taken you months or years to make).

What does she need *physically*? Have you ever asked her? Or is she is too uncomfortable to share her physical needs with you?

Have you listened sufficiently in your twenty-four hours with her to have some idea what she does need? Women long for a man who can share his feelings, so make an attempt to state how you *feel* on a matter (not just "what you think," once in awhile.) Then, and only then, may she feel both comfortable and safe enough to confide *her* feelings to you. Women have other women friends largely because they can confide in them. Can she confide in you and feel safe in your confidence?

Ask your lady about her physical and sexual needs. While many women may be intimidated and afraid to share their physical needs or lack of sexual fulfillment with their knight for fear that his manhood may be damaged or that he then may feel he cannot satisfy her and thus will leave the relationship. The true knight is not afraid to hear the truth. Only in knowing the truth does he know how she feels and have the opportunity to make things better for both of them. Women may be afraid to tell their men, and men, in all honesty, are many times afraid to hear the truth. But hearing the truth is the first step in making things the best they can be, both physically and emotionally, for both people. The quality of the physical relationship is only as good as both the man and the woman make it, and that is only possible by sharing your feelings. A man who can easily and openly share his deepest thoughts and feelings holds the key that can open the door to his lady's feelings, thoughts, and desires.

To the chivalrous knight: you have the key and you never even knew it! Open the door to your lady's heart and bravely seek out her deepest thoughts and desires. You are now nearing the 100th percentile of all knights.

Foreplay Is in *Daily Reminders of Love*

Do you remind your lady on a daily basis what she means to you? Flowers on no special date (flowers sent on an anniversary are wonderful, but are "expected." Send them on the third Tuesday this month—simply because that particular date has no special significance!) Remember her when you might not be expected to remember her. That's what she will always remember . . . .

Other daily reminders of love not mentioned earlier could include:

- A handwritten note left for her as you leave for work.

- Sending her a handwritten letter in the mail telling her that you love her.

- Sending or leaving tickets to a special show or event that she's been dying to see that has been sold out for months, along with a handwritten note from you.

- A gift certificate for a massage or all-day treatment at her favorite salon, with a note from you.

- Endless other ideas that your knightly creativity can generate.

How do you know if a gesture contains foreplay? Foreplay is in the constant reminder that she is the most important person in your life, and, if she is the mother of your children, in affirming how special she is as a wife and mother.

FOREPLAY: *WILLINGNESS TO MAKE A PUBLIC COMMITMENT TO HER AND TO YOUR RELATIONSHIP*

Holding hands in public, hugging and caressing, an innocent kiss (and sometimes a passionate kiss) are wonderful ways of letting her know that, "this knight is very happy with (and proud of) his lady—and he wants everyone to know it." We have all seen an older couple strolling along, hand in hand, and perhaps have commented on how wonderful it is to still be in love after all of their years together. We can learn something from those sightings! I've always believed that God sends us a message through those older couples. The purity of love between them that they demonstrate by holding hands and gazing into one another's eyes is reflective of God's own love for us. What we see by their actions and in their eyes is what He wanted for *all of us* to experience with each other when He created Adam and Eve.

My Grandmother's Funeral and My Grandfather's Chivalry

When my dear paternal grandmother, Minnie Milby, died in late 1988, I attended her funeral in Greensburg, Kentucky. Up until that day, my grandfather Johnny, who had been married to my grandmother for sixty-five years, had been a pillar of strength, having been employed in a sawmill for some fifty-five years and being a stout and powerful man, even at his advanced age.

The moment Grandpa Johnny arrived at the funeral home with my aunt and walked into the parlor and saw my grandmother lying there, this strong, wiry, yet still stout and powerful eighty-six-year-old crumbled, lunged towards me, and fell into my arms, sobbing bitterly. I will never forget that moment, when I held him as he cried. He felt like he weighed five pounds! This was a man that truly loved a woman—and had always loved her. The love I had never before realized he had for my grandmother was the type of love that I later wanted for my own life but had never known (until now). That day in 1988 helped set the standard for not only the type of woman I wanted in my own life, but how I needed to live my life if I was ever going to find "my lady." My life changed that day in a wonderful way, and I have never been the same since.

Johnny died some two years later after Minnie passed away. I saw him at his home in Greensburg shortly before his passing. At age eighty-eight, he was a tired and weary man in very poor health but with a peace and contentment in his eyes that clearly, yet quietly, whispered that he was ready to join Minnie in heaven. The look was unmistakable as I drove up and met him in his front yard, dribble running down his chin onto his wrinkled shirt, his clothing disheveled and in disarray. Although he was unkempt, the look in his eyes was that of a very wise and peaceful man who was passing something along to me through his eyes and his smile. I pray someone will see that in my eyes in my last days. It was the unmistakable look of someone with the peace, contentment, and wisdom of knowing he had lived a long, wonderful Christian life, who knew it, and who was totally prepared to meet the Lord. I have been envious of that look in Johnny's eyes ever since and have committed my life in working towards the moment when I have earned that same look. That was the last time I saw my grandfather alive.

My grandfather will always be a true knight in my eyes and in my heart—a man whom I suspect never knew much about knights, let alone anything at all about chivalry, at least nothing learned from a book. But he was a true *knight's knight* in terms of how he lived his life—a chivalrous Christian man and a major inspiration for the words you are reading now.

❦ FOREPLAY IS ABOUT *HOW SHE FEELS WHEN SHE'S WITH YOU*

Do you make your lady feel special? Has she ever told you that she feels special when she's with you or that she likes the way she feels about herself when she is with you? It's a wonderful thing to hear those words from the woman you love, because it lets you know you have done a good job of expressing your feelings of love toward her.

Further, her words let you know she has noticed your attentiveness to her and is expressing her appreciation of this, as well as her love toward you for doing so. The true knight makes his lady feel very special at all times and is totally attentive to her and her needs. He also never misses an opportunity to express his love for her by his gentlemanly and knightly actions:

- Opening the car door and gently supporting her arm as she enters and leaves the car.

- Seating her in the restaurant by taking her chair and standing behind it and easing the chair toward her as she adjusts in her seat.

- Rising from his chair as she rises from the table, then rising again as she returns (when possible).

- Dedicating 100 percent of your attention to her at all times (not looking at other ladies).

- Taking her coat and helping her on and off with her coat.

- Carrying your lady across a mud puddle in the rain (Yes, I've done that!)

- Fixing dinner for your lady and others in honor of her.

- Offering her your handkerchief before she actually asks you for it; i.e., anticipating her needs.

- Planning special activities or surprises for her (women love to be surprised, and especially love a man who likes to surprise his lady; in other words, a man of mystery).

- Being a gentleman of discretion and good taste in public settings.

FOREPLAY IS IN MAKING HONESTY A HALLMARK OF YOUR LIVES TOGETHER

There's an old saying that, "If you always tell the truth, you never have to try to remember what you said." No truer words were ever spoken. And it's never truer than in a relationship with your lady. Today's true knight makes honesty his policy in all things, which is also one of the ten tenets of the "Code of Chivalry":

"Thou shalt never lie, and shall remain faithful to thy pledged word."

An honest man is a man who can be respected in all things, including relationships. While discretion in some things may be a good thing, honesty in the knight's relationship with his lady is essential—for a relationship without honest expression and truth is baseless and cannot stand. Be honest in your feelings, thoughts, emotions, and concerns, and your relationship will only be stronger for it. Further, as the Greek philosopher Diogenes noted, "an honest and sincere man is very hard to find," and your lady's respect for you, in being one, will grow daily.

❦FOREPLAY IS IN YOUR OPEN WILLINGNESS IN MAKING A LIFETIME COMMITMENT TO HER

Men spend the better part of their lives running from relationships with women. In our teens and twenties, we're in our "hunting" mode, living lives of open conquest like so many "Napoleons" with no worlds left to conquer. We hurt the ladies in our lives by our insincerity, and, in all honesty, are also hurt ourselves much of the time.

The mark of true maturity and wisdom for today's knight is in his ability to openly and honestly make a lifetime commitment to a proper lady. I'm not sure *why* we men run from this moment, but, many times, we do. Maybe it stems from our biological makeup in that we're hunters by nature and don't like giving up the hunt or conquest for the outcome of the next "hunting expedition." A lot of it is simply that we don't want to give up our freedom as men to do *what* we want, *where* we want, and *when* we want. We feel that commitment to one woman takes something important from us, and that it somehow makes us weaker men. Truth be told, the right woman makes us an infinitely stronger man, while the wrong women in our lives break us down and make us weaker and more dysfunctional. The key lies in today's knight, in his wisdom, taking the time to find the right lady and not just "settling" for any old "lady-in-waiting." Too many of us, both knights and ladies, have *settled* with disastrous results. There are a lot of potential partners out there who are very *wrong* for you, yet, they will seek you out for wrong reasons of their own, reasons other than true love and commitment.

While the timing of the discovery of a true love may vary widely by individual, the knight knows when he has found his true love and sees that he has found someone worth being with for the rest of his days. He feels a comfort and an unexplainable peace of mind and confidence, all wrapped up within an unbounded love that cannot be fully verbalized. It also intrigues him and begs to be further explored.

The truly strong man is not the least bit afraid to make a total commitment of marriage to his lady; in fact, he becomes excited about that possibility and wants it just as much as she may. The most tangible demonstration of commitment that a man can make to a lady is through the proposal of marriage, with an engagement ring being the accepted evidence of that sincere commitment. The man that can make a total commitment to his lady in the form of a proposal and subsequent marriage is regarded both by her and other women alike as a strong and desirable man worthy of respect and admiration. Further, his open expression of love leads his relationship with his lady into more intimate waters—making the relationship more solid and rewarding.

FOREPLAY IS IN *THE SELFLESSNESS OF PUTTING HER BEFORE YOURSELF*

The Bible teaches us that as the men of our houses, we are to place our wives before ourselves and to honor and cherish them. The very Bible-based marriage vows we speak during the wedding ceremony note that we are to: "love, honor, and cherish till death do us part." As knights, can we do any less for the lady so essential to the happiness in our lives?

The knight puts his lady before himself in all things—her comfort, her security, her wishes and desires, her concerns, her tastes and preferences, and her wants and needs. Those things that are important to her are foremost in his mind. Enough said. Today's intelligent, intuitive knight can fill in the blanks here.

FOREPLAY IS IN *THE ONGOING DEMONSTRATION OF YOUR LOVE*

The biggest mistake men make either in a long-term relationship before marriage or after marriage is in taking their ladies for granted. We stop "dating" and allow the excitement and the spark to die. All relationships need constant refueling, and your own will be no exception, I assure you. Today's knight keeps the fire alive by continuing to "court" his lady through courtly behaviors such as these:

- Making dates with his lady, whether married or not.

- Constant reminders of love and that you are still very much attracted to her.

- Constant verbal comments and physical gestures of how beautiful she is to you and what she means to you.

- Planning romantic getaways as often as possible.

- Not letting children keep you from continuing to date or from having that romantic connection.

- Gifts, including the same types of expensive gifts you gave when you first met or before you were married (diamonds and jewelry, flowers, cards, etc.).

- Manners: opening car doors, seating your lady, helping with her coat, etc.

Marriage, or the mere fact that you and your lady have been together for a long time, does not excuse the knight from his gentlemanly responsibilities and obligations, nor from the expectation that he will continue his courtly behavior within a committed relationship. *How are you doing here?*

❧FOREPLAY IS IN *BEING WARM, CARING, AND CONSIDERATE*

We men can sometimes be rather out-of-touch when it comes to empathizing with women. We may tend not to see things from the lady's perspective, and, as a result, miss the proverbial mark. It's as much incorporating the golden rule as anything else: "Treat her as you would have her treat you." Do you like it when your lady seems insensitive to your needs or appears disinterested in what you have to say? Well, she feels the same way when we would-be knights seem to be tuned out when she is sharing her thoughts on the day or wants to discuss something with you. We've spoken of the importance of listening before; suffice it to say that a good knight is a good listener!

Further, a good knight is sensitive to the reaction his lady is likely to have to his words and actions and thus tempers his behavior in respect to her feelings and likely reactions. He cares about her feelings and is careful not to say or do anything that might be misunderstood or that might hurt or anger her. He is considerate of her wants and needs and demonstrates his interest in seeing her happy. While we as men all stumble and fall from time to time, the knight makes a conscious effort to be warm, caring, considerate, and in touch with his lady's needs. If he makes a mistake from time to time, it will thus be more quickly and easily forgiven and result in a lesser *withdrawal* from her emotional bank account.

FOREPLAY IS IN *KNOWING HER SIZES, COLORS, PREFERENCES*

It goes without saying that the chivalrous knight's knowledge of his lady's sizes should consist of knowing more than her brassiere size. While your lady may not be especially excited about your knowing that her dress size just went from a size ten to a size twelve, you can and should be aware of her sizes. It's the mark of a knowledgeable knight. In particular, knowing her ring size, dress size, shoe size, and general sizes for things such as robes, gowns, and other items adds to your knightly stature. It's also very good to know the sizes of more intimate items, as it shows your awareness and interest in her. However, temper your zeal and knightly enthusiasm according to your lady's sensitivity to weight, fluctuations in weight, and other considerations.

Things you should know (at minimum):

- Her ring size.

- Her shoe size.

- Her body style (women are built differently; that is, they have different body styles: short, tall, long-waisted versus short-waisted, buxom versus flat-chested; yet each is beautiful in her own way, so choose fashions that compliment her and her body style.)

- Her dress and outfit size (and how types of fashions and sizes differ by designer and manufacturer, even by the sizing practices of various stores; i.e., Casual Corner versus Petite Sophisticate, versus Macy's, etc. Example: a size twelve in one suit may be cut small, while another size twelve might be cut differently by another designer, and so on. In other words, a size twelve at one store or by one designer might not be exactly the same as a size twelve from another. Further, and listen, men, this is important: women's body styles are all different, and because the ladies are built differently, a style that looks really great on one lady may not be as flattering on another woman with a different body style, or with an outfit from a different designer or store. So, be aware before purchasing a gift in the wrong size or style).

- Blouse and sweater sizes (same as above on women's styles, stores, and body sizes).

- Her pant size (same as above).

- Size of undergarments (bras, panties, and the style and fabric she prefers).

- Brand/style and size of panty hose.

- Her favorite perfume, makeup brand, etc.

- Her favorite colors, in order of preference.

- The color of her eyes and her "colorization season" (Is she a fall, a winter, a spring, or a summer?)

- Her approximate height and weight.

If you don't know something, such as her ring size, and are hesitant to ask her, simply borrow the ring, have it sized, and bring it back the same day. As for clothes, take a look at the tag sizes when you have a quiet opportunity to do so, and write them down in a safe place (your wallet?) for future reference. Knowing her colors and other statistics unique to her reinforces your knightly interest in the exquisite individual and very special lady in your life.

❧FOREPLAY IS IN *TAKING TIME TO BE A GOOD LISTENER*

Three simple rules here: listen, listen, and then, listen. A good knight knows how to listen both to what is being said, as well as how to "fill in the blanks" of what is left unsaid.

Foreplay is in every compliment, no matter how small. Many of us men have little appreciation for the lengths women go to in appearing before us as beautifully as they do.

The time it takes to have their hair done and the thought and deliberation that goes into trying a new hairstyle, a new outfit, nails, new makeup products, etc., all take a tremendous amount of time, research, and dedication.

Unfortunately, many vassals take all this for granted. Further, we have no concept of the damage and devastation we cause her when we: a) don't notice at all, or, b) make some careless statement, such as:

- "I don't like it!"

- "That makes you look fat!"

- "I don't like your hair!"

- "Why did you go and do that?"

Women love compliments—those that are many and that come often. We knights need to appreciate all of the efforts our ladies go to in looking as beautiful as they do. A simple compliment that we *like something* says that we not only notice, but that we appreciate our ladies and what they do and how they add joy and pleasure to our lives. This also reveals our sensitivity to and our caring of them and their needs. Remember, she is beautiful to you. Remind her at every opportunity.

❧ FOREPLAY IS IN *SHARING HOW YOU FEEL*

It has always been difficult for many would-be knights to share their feelings because it was ingrained in most of us from boyhood that we were to be strong men; we should not cry, that to share our feelings suggested that we were weak or too feminine, that work and career were the only determinants of success, and so on, *ad nauseum*. Because of the indoctrination received from parents, relatives, peers, and acquaintances over our lifetimes, we as men, not only feel uncomfortable in sharing feelings, but, even worse, don't even know *how* to share our feelings, or at least, how to share them well. Rather, we may go through life numb and, as Mr. Natural used to say, "just passing through," without being able to relate in a compassionate, tender way as a well-rounded, qualified knight should.

A man who is able to share his thoughts and feelings candidly and honestly to the lady in his life is a rare find, and one that your lady will want to keep for herself. If you (like many aspiring squires) lack skill in this area, speak up. Asking a few key questions can initiate a process of sharing that will at least get you some good practice!

❧ FOREPLAY IS IN *ASKING WHAT SHE WANTS/ NEEDS AND SHARING WHAT YOU WANT/NEED*

One of the most difficult things for a man to do is to ask a woman what she wants. The female gender can be challenging enough to understand, anyway, let alone having our would-be knights opening up a potential Pandora's Box by asking such provocative questions as, "Honey, what do you really want?"

Her first thoughts might be: *Is he really interested in what I want? What does he mean, what do I want? What is he really trying to say to me? Or, What's wrong? Why is he asking me what I want? Doesn't he know already? Why, that insensitive jerk!*

However, in order to be a true chivalrous knight of the twenty-first century, the question must be asked. Still in all, and this is also important, gents, if we have been listening to our ladies all along, this question and the potential risks associated with asking the question might be a non-issue, don't you think? All the more reason to "Listen, and listen tight," as "The Duke" used to say.

If you've listened intently to her over time, you likely understand what she wants and needs. However, if you haven't listened as well as you should have, or if its early in the relationship and you simply want to start out by just asking outright, asking her what she wants and feels in and of itself demonstrates an incredible sensitivity and interest that ninety-nine percent of the rest of men on planet earth have not demonstrated. So, you're already in select company!

However, if you ask the question, be prepared to hear the answer. You may hear something that you're either not prepared to hear or something for which you are in no way prepared to provide a response. If you're going to ask the question, anticipate her wants and needs and be prepared to know how you will respond to what she says in reply. You love her, or you would not be asking. And, if you *do* love her as you say you do, then the answer is as important to you as it is to her. Consider her responses, so that you can begin responding to the needs and wants she identifies right away. Her wants and needs could be of a sexual, emotional, and/or communicative nature. Are you prepared to hear any or all of the above and ready to respond to each or all?

Keep in mind that any good pairing or marriage is an "equal opportunity relationship." Too often, one or both partners in a marriage or relationship feel that they are obliged to give considerable ground in order to "help make the marriage work." This has been proven to be a losing strategy. Rather, be courageous! It's more than OK to share with her your knightly needs, just as much as it's more than OK for her to share her wants and needs with you. In fact, if you *don't* do this, your marriage or relationship can be in serious jeopardy over time. If your actions contribute to your giving up your identity, the relationship isn't working, period. You cannot be happy, and, honestly, neither can your spouse or mate because he/she doesn't recognize the person you've become, or, more seriously, may no longer respect you for giving up your own identity so easily. Be compassionate and caring, but be yourself. Your lady will respect you for it.

I'm not saying that compromise isn't relevant; on the contrary, compromise is both necessary and healthy in a godly relationship characterized by two people who both love each other and who have established open lines of communication. The problem occurs and communication breaks down when one or both partners *overcompensate* by giving up "too much" of themselves. Resentment can form, and partners lose the ability to recognize or understand each other. Today's chivalrous knight works diligently to foster and maintain open communication with his lady and initiates every effort to share his feelings, while creating a loving and safe domestic respite for her so that she feels safe, free, and comfortable to be herself and to share her feelings.

Foreplay Is in *Being Attentive, Every Day*

A knight should never let a day go by without giving his lady his undivided attention in everything he says and does. The good knight will become so accomplished in his attentiveness toward his lady that it will become second nature, yet, never be taken lightly and always undertaken at the highest priority.

Simply put, give her your undivided attention when you are with her; treat her with loving courtesy and respect every moment you have with her because life is fleeting, and the Lord may call you home at anytime, and let her know as many times as possible each day that she is foremost in your mind.

Foreplay Is in *Respect for Her Family and Friends*

Only an idiot demonstrates a lack of respect for a lady's family and friends. It's quite probable that you came on the scene later than her mother, father, siblings, and extended family, so her feelings for them are strong and important. As for friends, the wise knight knows that women form very powerful emotional bonds with others, especially other women, so respect her friendships with both genders and remember that they are *her* relationships, thus are important to her. If they are important to her, they are important to the true chivalrous knight. Showing a lack of respect for family and friends is simply showing a lack of respect for her.

Even so, your lady should also be attentive to your tireless efforts and demonstrate that you are important to her. The knight, while doing what he can to respect his lady's relationships, should also expect to receive the respect of her family and friends, particularly if he has shown his colors as a true knight of class and taste. If she doesn't, maybe she is unworthy of your knightly charms. A discussion of mutuality here may be in order.

❦FOREPLAY IS IN *BEING SUPPORTIVE OF HER CAREER*

Most women become intensely involved in their careers, in part due to the financial necessity of simply doing a good job and, in part, due to old chauvinistic policies and social norms that require that, "a woman must work twice as hard for the same pay as a man." Women can sometimes be abused in the workplace by employers who take advantage of a woman's marital status, traditionally lower pay, or pre-employment economic situation. In other cases, women love what they do and are very successful, so much so that their work becomes their passion, and in some cases, the focal point of their lives. There may not be a spouse or a significant partner (or anyone worth counting on in their marriage) in their lives to depend upon.

The true knight recognizes the importance of his lady's career to her world and the reasons behind its importance to her. Not only does he understand; he shows his willingness to help (but not *hover* over her) by supporting her work, helping out and showing support by attending company functions, being supportive of demanding schedules, and just being "at arm's reach" when called upon. Again, being supportive of her career and of what it means to her life is showing your love and respect for her, and sets you apart as a unique man.

❦Foreplay Is in Knowing the Difference Between Making Love, Being Loving, Being in Love—and in Letting Her Know that You Know the Difference

The knight that knows the difference between *making love, being loving,* and *being in love* and is able to move between each with ease is a man who knows himself. First and foremost, today's knight is keenly aware that the concept of foreplay transcends all three elements of his relationship with his lady.

Again, foreplay is a 24/7 proposition and encompasses every thought, word, and action the knight incorporates into his life and his relationship. Some thoughts on the key differences are:

1. *Making Love*

   The art of creating an environment of physical intimacy through thoughtful gestures, touching, and physical activity is not only just before and during lovemaking but at all other times. The man's ability to "prepare and excite" his lady and to "create an ongoing and intense anticipation of and desire for intimacy" every day, day in and day out, through caring words, reaffirmation of love, tender touches, intimate conversations and sharing, and activities outside of the actual moment of lovemaking are all key components. In making love, he is patient, understanding, humble, and responsive to her and her needs and is willing to ensure her pleasure at the compromise of his own satisfaction. Foreplay from a sexual perspective is the slow, deliberate development of the lady's sexual desire and readiness for lovemaking through attentiveness to her unique needs for those intimate movements, touches, caresses, and manual stimulation that are most likely to deliver the maximum pleasure to her and to best prepare her for orgasm. Intercourse is the manifestation of the act, taking place when foreplay has achieved its objective of maximizing his lady's pleasure and at the moment when she is most ready to achieve orgasm.

2. *Being Loving*

"Exhibiting your love, interest in, and affection for your lady, 24 hours a day, 7 days a week, in all that you do, from kind words of love, to gestures of servitude (taking out the garbage, washing her car, baby-sitting the kids while she has a "free day" or a "girl's night out," etc.), or that of being patient and understanding when she has experienced a bad day and all she needs is for you to listen," is the core definition of being a loving man. Foreplay also applies here in a different context as you show your love for her in your thoughts, words, and actions while creating and maintaining a safe nest for her. You love her and you demonstrate your love every day, not only to her, but to everyone either of you happen to interact with during the course of the day.

3. *Being in Love*

If you're "in love," it shows in all that you say and do. Foreplay is evident here, too, as everything you say and do serves to reinforce your love for her. It is also manifested in how you express your love for her, in and out of the bedroom. You tell her that you love her and that you're in love with her, often and in many ways. Your daily life, activities, and Christian values are abundantly evident in your every move, and you reassure her regularly that she is the most important person in your life—and that you thank God for her every day.

If you clearly perceive the above differences, you have reached the 100th percentile and are a completely chivalrous knight! You are rare, exceptional, and a true romantic—lost in another time and place—the desire of all women and the envy of all men!

❧FOREPLAY IS *EVERYTHING YOU SAY AND DO . . . EVERY DAY*

Foreplay is in fact everything you say and do, everyday, and your every word and action contributes to the strength or weakness of your relationship with your lady. Use caution and discretion, and pick your "thoughts" and words wisely so that they elevate and please, and do not detract or harm your lady.

Make it a point to "endeavor to persevere" by sculpting each and every word and action as a post-impressionist master would use every stroke of his or her brush to create just the right scene in his or her mind's eye. Your life is a painting: do not leave out even one brush stroke, either in your own painting, or in the painting you help create for others, especially your lady.

Make everything you say and do something which originates "in love," or leave what is best left unsaid alone until you can approach it with kindness.

❦FOREPLAY IS IN *REINFORCING THAT SHE'S THE ONLY ONE, AND LIVING IT*

If you have followed even most of the above mentioned items, you are doing your knightly duty in reinforcing to your *lady faire* that she is the only one for you, that she is essential to your life and to your every breath, and that she is "your life." Having said it, you need now only to live your thoughts and words by living your commitment to her. If you are already married, reassure her, "date" her, pamper her, surprise her, treat her, court her as only a knight of your stature could, protect her, "rescue her from life and its problems," and "listen to and for her." Be a man in the truest sense, and you will be a chivalrous knight and the man that God must have envisioned for us all to be when he created Adam.

She is your Eve . . . created to be your earthly companion, partner, and life-mate. Love her, counsel her, care for her and about her, advise her, and let her advise you, elevate her above yourself as the Bible has taught us to do as men. Honor and cherish her, respect her, and, above all, place God at the center of your relationship so that you ensure your togetherness *en Paradisium* with Jesus Christ and God, the Father. So shall you be a valiant knight, stalwart and true!

Chapter Eight

HAVING A KNIGHT'S MENTALITY IN EVERYDAY THINGS

Talking a good game is one thing. Living the life of a true, chivalrous knight is another entirely. Take a minute and think about it. Are you living your life according to the values and precepts we've been discussing? And, if not, *why not?* Maybe you've convinced yourself that it wouldn't really matter, that nothing would be different even if you did adopt more chivalrous lifestyle habits. But let me ask you this: do you really believe that you have done *all in your power* and capacity to make your world a better place for your lady, your family, society, and your nation? Or could you improve your walk and talk in life and the effort you're now making? Can you state with assurance that your life is everything it *could* be? What would that be like?

Walking the talk is a difficult challenge for anyone. A good example of this is what we in the Baptist church used to label the "Sunday Morning Christian." The SMC, as I'll call him, would come to church on Sunday, appear pious and faithful, and upon leaving the building would immediately disregard all that he had heard and learned and revert back to a secular lifestyle. By the way, the SMC does not limit his membership to the Baptists; there are SMC's in all denominations and churches. My point here is that "talking the talk" is easy while "walking the talk" and making the effort to implement Christ's teachings in our everyday lives as Christian knights is the ultimate challenge, yet well worth the effort.

Walking the walk in our daily attitudes about others, in our Christian stewardship and financial giving—both to the church and to God's work abroad, and to others in need—is challenging. Practicing humility, showing loyalty and commitment to our lady, aggressively defending our families against evil, and contributing to society and defending our nation while showing compassion for others, as the earliest knights were charged to do, are not easy assignments for a man.

What is so obvious and so exciting, however, is that these principles of chivalry and honor are absolutely pertinent and relevant to our lives today, whether we are practicing Christians or not. Yet if we are Christians, the keeping of these knightly principles and commandments makes us not only better, stronger men who are more desirable to our ladies, but also makes us truer Christians, as well. The principles outlined in the knightly Codes of Conduct were forged in the cradle of Christian faith and doctrine, so doesn't it stand to reason that they would be just as reliable and relevant guideposts for our walk of faith today?

If some of you are not presently Christians and have not yet found Christ as your personal Savior, would not the pursuit of these God-based principles for living present the possibility of being led closer to Christ and to the fellowship of His Church? In fact, uncovering the Christian-based principles set in place at the onset of the Crusades some one thousand years ago was an essential motivation in the vision for this book—that, in so doing, these principles might not only enhance the Christian experience of men who are practicing Christians, but might also bring others to Christ.

Ah, chivalrous knight, hear this! If you learn nothing else as a knight living in this century, learn that these principles are timeless, that they not only set you apart as a special man to the lady in your life, but also serve a far more significant and eternal purpose—that of bringing you closer to God and to the reality of your spending eternity with Him!

How "Being Considerate" Can Become Second Nature

Being a considerate man will become *second nature* to the chivalrous knight once the principles of the knightly Codes of Conduct (stated above) are placed into practice. Your thoughtfulness will not only add joy to the lives of those you touch, but the warmth and tenderness of the responses you receive back from others will far outweigh the effort you expend to provide whatever knightly service, positive compliments, or comfort you bestow upon them.

Be considerate in your thoughts and words—not only in what you *say* but in the manner in which you deliver your words. Be considerate, too, in your acts of kindness, such as opening the door for a complete stranger, helping someone you don't know cross the street, or buying Girl Scout cookies you may never eat just to help out a little girl who is doing something good and honorable and trying to sell her quota. Offer to buy a homeless man sitting at a gas station a sandwich at the same time that you buy your own, or, do without, even when it hurts, so that someone else can "have." The list of such small "considerate acts" can and should be lengthy at the end of your days. I hope so—for your sake and for mine. In short, a life of selflessness, honor in the treatment of all men, humility, and unqualified Christian charity is the very cornerstone of a true, chivalrous knight! He grows in stature and character by his selfless acts of kindness toward others.

On a Personal Note

Knights, it took me some *fifty years* to get it right and to qualify as a chivalrous knight in the Christian sense, although I imagine I had possessed many knightly virtues for years. "Practice makes perfect," and pays dividends in time. The important point is that I did finally *get it*. Many men may never, *ever* get it and will pass into eternity never having realized what this brief life that God granted us was even all about. Only a very few, a lucky few I think, are ever blessed with the knowledge of what is truly important. And those are the ones who seek it out like silver and search for it as gold.

I paid what I used to think was a dear price, both financially and emotionally, in suffering through and emerging from two failed marriages in order to become one of the "lucky few." But as my spiritual strength increases and my walk with God intensifies; I now realize that what I gave up was *nothing,* yet what I received in return is indeed priceless. I understand, now, that a Christian man is, must be, and must remain a humble man, one who places *nothing* ahead of God, else he will lose that misplaced treasure . . . and himself, as well.

BEING BOTH STRONG *AND* SENSITIVE

It's OK to be both strong (masculine) and sensitive at the same time. Don't believe all the propaganda otherwise that has been beaten into men's heads over the years by society and the media advertising machine. You *can* be both strong and sensitive. In fact, finding the balance of the two opposite traits is highly desirable; doing so can lead to discovering the freedom of a "new and happier you." I find the knight's code can help here.

A knightly man who exhibits strength and self-assurance while at the same time being able to reveal his sensitive nature is a man better able to communicate his thoughts and feelings, making him a rare, highly prized, and attractive potential mate. *Try it!* The chivalrous knight is both strong and sensitive, and enjoys the sweet favor of his lady.

Chapter Nine

TODAY'S KNIGHT— WARRIOR, PRINCE, CHEF, AND STEWARD

Today's chivalrous knight is a true twenty-first century man, yet he reflects many of the traits of the original knights of a millennium ago. Today's man/knight is the picture of a *complete male:* a balanced man of integrity, Christian faith, and moral fortitude displaying class, manners, and discretion. He is a man wise both in financial matters and in matters of the heart, one who reasons thoroughly before he acts, yet a man who is also a warrior at heart—with the courage and selflessness to defend his *lady faire*, castle, family, friends, God, and country.

Men of selfish motivation and limited vision are foreigners to the true knight. Our knight is not selfish, ill-mannered, crude, rude, profane, insensitive, abusive, or exclusively preoccupied with sex. The "cave man mentality" has no place in the heart of the chivalrous knight. Rather, the knight of today exhibits a wondrous combination of masculinity, education, style, grace, culture, maturity, perceptiveness, intelligence, mystery, covert sensuality, unpredictability, and stately elegance—a man of boundless kindness and selflessness. Today's knight is a man of honor treating others with compassion and generosity, without prejudice, and one who does not hide or diminish his Christian code of ethics and belief in God before man. Rather, he actively seeks God and His wisdom and strives to reach his lady, his children, his family and relatives, his friends, and everyone his life touches with the message of Jesus Christ and His Salvation.

Today's knight is a wondrous mix of Christian values, wisdom, grace, style, and sensuality. And yes, a Christian man can be very sexy, indeed. *Why?* His values alone make him a rarity in this age of blatant debauchery, and that's exceptionally sexy. Further, he's sexy because he *gets it;* he gets the true meaning of life, which makes him an ideal mate and a life partner for any wise lady—as today's woman knows. He's a loving, caring, Christian man who is sensitive yet quietly strong, secure in himself and in his eternal destiny. This man "has it all, and has it together," as we used to say years ago.

One final note: being "classy" isn't something you can manufacture or project as being the *real* you. When it comes to knighthood, you either "are," or you "are not." The quality manner in which we as men will increasingly lead our lives as we practice the disciplines in the knight's Code of Honor will become an automatic way of life and should not be in any way *contrived* or forced. To live according to principle is to live without pretense. It's the way you *really* live your life, who you are "when nobody's watching." End of discussion.

Today's Knight and the Humanities

How many art exhibits and art museums have you visited lately? Would you know an R.C. Gorman or J.D. Challenger from a Picasso? Would you know a tier II postimpressionist master from a tier I? Have you seen *Phantom of the Opera? Porgy and Bess? Les Miserables?* Have you ever attended the opera? Did you like it? Have you attended a philharmonic concert in the last five years? How about a lecture by a leading author at the local college or university? How many pop concerts have you seen lately? Have you limited your cultural exploits to Eminem, Britney Spears, and others, or do you enjoy all musicians and artists, including the ones mentioned? Are you thinking, *What's the difference?* Allow me to share from experience my own discovery of how the humanities can enrich a life.

Until my senior year in high school I had never been exposed to *any* of the humanities; they were a rarity in my home. During my senior year, I reluctantly took a Humanities class with Mrs. Kummer, who had been my junior English teacher and someone with whom I had not gotten along well. During that year, I was exposed to many forms of the Humanities: the arts, literature, opera, orchestral concerts, fine art, etc. Suddenly, my life changed. In fact, I did so well in the humanities during college that my professor offered me a full graduate scholarship in the subject. In short, I would not be the man I am today had it not been for Mrs. Kummer (God bless you, and thank you, dear teacher!)

If you have not exposed yourself to the arts, to literature, and to the wealth of music (classical, jazz, and popular), there's *no time like the present* to do so. Today's astute knight has a variety of interests in the arts and humanities. Being aware of what's going on in the creative arts is part of your mystery and appeal to the lady of your life. But don't "study up" just to please her. Do it for yourself, for the opportunity to grow as a person and as a thoughtful, caring, cultured, well-bred man. Get beyond a focus on self and broaden your horizons; you may be surprised at the things you enjoy! *How do you begin?*

Make it a point to seek out and attend each of the following at least once during the coming year:

- One philharmonic concert.

- One operatic performance (*La Boheme, La Traviata, The Barber of Seville*, etc.).

- Two jazz performances (Richard Elliott, Al Jarreau, Kirk Whalum, Ramsey Lewis, Dave Koz).

- Two Broadway Shows (*Les Miserables, The Producers, Rent*);

- Two art exhibits (New York, Los Angeles, or the *Guggenheim at the Venetian* in Las Vegas).

- One university lecture by a leading author.

- One ballet performance (every man should see *The Nutcracker* at least once in his life!)

- The Three Tenors (Domingo, Carreras, Pavarotti).

- Andrea Bocelli (a wonderful tenor).

- One Picasso or other exhibit by a widely recognized master (Rembrandt, Monet, Pizarro).

Exposing himself to a variety of arts and literature will make today's knight grow ever stronger as both an individual and as a sensitive, loving companion and soulmate to his lady.

THE IMPORTANCE OF A SENSE OF HUMOR

When women are asked what are among the most attractive traits in a man or potential mate, a "sense of humor" is consistently mentioned as one of the most important characteristics in an ideal man. When asked what makes the man in their life so attractive, the statement that, "he makes me laugh" is also frequently mentioned as a major factor in the man's attractiveness and appeal. While we are not all *born comedians* with the immense talent of Richard Pryor, Jerry Seinfeld, Paul Rodriquez, Jeff Foxworthy or Robin Williams, we can ensure that comedy and the ability to laugh at odd circumstances (and ourselves) are readily accessible in our lives.

What do you do to bring laughter and a comedic twist into your relationship with your lady? Do you send her cards with a humorous twist that will give her a smile? Do you see that the two of you are exposed to comedy and comedic artists that make you both laugh? Laughter has been proven not only to be fun, but good for you, as well, as it provides a major outlet for stress. Make sure that you provide a venue for laughter, both in your activities and in your daily lives.

What makes you laugh? What makes her laugh and smile? Are you doing enough smiling and laughing? If yes, how can you encourage more of the same? And if not, how can you bring more laughter into your knightly life and into her life, as well?

A sense of humor can also relate to how easily you deal with life; i.e., how you seem not to be bothered by life's problems but shrug them off with ease. Further, having a sense of humor about life and its challenges shows strength, stability, confidence, and resolve that is easily readable by the lady in your life. Your good humor also makes you fun to be around as you're happy and capable of having a good time. In other words, don't take things *too seriously,* and make sure that you establish a place for fun and relaxation, while having a light yet responsible attitude about daily life and the little "hiccups" that occur each day.

The Knight as Protector

We have dedicated a great deal of time to issues other than the knight's role as defender and protector of his lady, his family, his castle, and his society. However, the very basis for knighthood and the Code of Chivalry a thousand years ago was for the protection and perpetuation of the Christian faith against those who would seek to destroy it. The knight's role as a *protector* can be viewed from several levels: protection of his lady, protection of his family and castle, and protection of his country.

A. Protecting His Lady

   While the true knight has many duties, a primary responsibility and one that the knight must take very seriously is in the protection of his lady. While the nature of protection may have changed since early knighthood, today's knight still willingly accepts the charge of protecting his lady from the forces that would place her in harm's way. Today's knight protects his lady in several ways—providing financial security, physical security, and emotional security.

B. Financial Security

Today's knight strives to ensure that the financial stability of his castle is sound and that financial decisions regarding both saving and spending are made responsibly. He looks well to the safety and security of his home and especially to his lady's present and future security. While life's misfortunes do occur and force hardships upon us all, today's knight does whatever he can to foster a safe and secure financial setting.

Being a good steward with God's gifts is an essential characteristic of a truly sincere and responsible knight. A common rule practiced among many Christian denominations is that of 10/10/80, a rule for managing God's financial gifts, explained as follows:

- The first 10 percent of your gross earnings is immediately returned to God through tithing.

- The second 10 percent of your gross earnings is placed in savings for the security of your castle.

- The remaining 80 percent is used for daily living expenses.

Being a good steward is not only appropriate for creating and maintaining a secure home for your *lady faire,* but it is God's commandment. The Book of Malachi states it very clearly:

> Should people cheat God? Yet you have cheated me! But you ask, "What do you mean? When did we ever cheat you? You have cheated me of the tithes and offerings due to me. You are under a curse, for your whole nation has been cheating me. Bring all the tithes into the storehouse, so there will be enough food in my temple. If you do," says the Lord Almighty, "I will open the windows of heaven for you. I will pour out a blessing so great you won't have enough room to take it in! Try it! Let me prove it to you!" (Malachi 3:8–10 NLT)

So, financial responsibility is not only the right thing to do as a knight, but concurrently is the right thing to do as a Christian man and protector of one's lady and household.

C. Physical Security

Protecting your lady from physical harm can take many forms: from simply protecting her from being bumped or jabbed as you walk along together, to the installation of a home security system so that she feels safe and secure at all times, or to physically defending her in the presence of real and imminent personal injury or danger. The knight must take into consideration every aspect of his lady and his home's safety, because the knight's family is his most important responsibility. The knight must also be forever prepared to protect his lady or family at all times without consideration for his own safety.

D. Emotional Security

"How safe is your lady physically?" is an all-important question, but even more importantly, "How safe does she *feel?*" This question relates not only to physical safety but to financial safety, as well. Yet there's one additional, critical element that we as men may many times overlook. It deals with the emotional safety she feels (or doesn't feel) in her everyday life. I've always believed that the absence of this emotional security may lead to *insecurity* in both men and women and could be partly responsible for extramarital affairs among couples.

We neglect to reaffirm our love for our lady to our own peril when we allow our sensitive "flower" to go bone dry in the *emotional planter,* so to speak. Instead, she should be constantly reminded and reassured that not only do you love her, but that you'll *always* love her and be there for her, no matter what circumstances may arise. In light of all she means to you, could you really do less? Not if you were operating in true wisdom.

While men are "emotional camels," storing up a month's supply of emotional "water" and capable of going weeks on end without a refill of loving refreshment (such as a verbal *I love you* from her), our lady isn't made that way. She doesn't function well in an emotional "desert." The inner security that comes from hearing the words, "I love you" each and every day gives her the assurance that you as her knight/protector are operating from a position of committed, living love and are dedicated long-term to your lady, to Christ, and to His Body, His Church.

It's our duty as chivalrous knights to continually replenish our lady's emotional stores, ever-reminding her that we love her so that her emotional storehouse is full and overflowing. If we are responsible in so doing, have we not ensured the stability of our ladies and our homes, much as the knights of old before us did? Further, we shall have done God's bidding and will have the hope of homes and lives richly blessed by His love and grace.

❧ LIVING A CHIVALROUS LIFE WITH GOD AT THE CENTER

This might be a good time to point out that for both men and women, their faith in Jesus Christ must be at the center of a marriage in order for the marriage to have a sound foundation. This Christ-centered underpinning only enhances the ability of the couple to allow their emotional intimacy to grow and blossom into something real, intense, and impenetrable. Some are fortunate enough to learn this early on in life and thus enjoy a lifetime happy marriage, rich with memories and blessings, with both partners secure in their eternal destiny. Others make the mistake, as I did, of entering into relationships without God at the center and/or for the wrong reasons—thus experiencing broken and emotionally devastating periods of divorce (two divorces in my case), betrayal, and destruction.

Again, it took me almost my entire fifty years or so of life to recognize this and to make things right with God. But, then again, *better late than never.* "God whispers to us in our pleasure; He shouts to us in our pain," as C.S. Lewis said, and some folks are just a little bit *deafer,* I imagine.

❧THE ALLURE OF BEING A GREAT COOK

Have you ever noticed how women swoon at the sight of Emeril, Wolfgang Puck, or other well-known TV chefs as they prepare their latest exotic dish? These gentlemen are true chivalrous knights! Or have you caught the wishful reactions of women when another woman shares the story of "her" man, who took the time and special care to prepare a meal just for her? Face it, knights, men who can cook at all are sexy and rare, while men who can prepare gourmet meals are worthy of tomorrow's editorial column. Besides, many women don't like to cook (or don't know *how* to cook and aren't the least bit interested in learning, either). A man who cooks happily is, again, an interesting possibility.

Being a great cook is not difficult. Just follow the recipes in your favorite cookbook. Taking the time to prepare a special meal for your lady places the knight in a special category. You *care* . . . and are taking the time to do something really special for her. It's another "surprise," a gift of love. And, quite honestly, cooking is a lot of fun—a terrific diversion from our normal routine. The best part is seeing the smile and look of appreciation on your lady's face as she begins to enjoy your wonderful culinary treat.

Do it for her first of all, but *enjoy* the experience. Creative cooking only adds to your skills' repertoire and resume as a chivalrous knight. You might even think about taking a cooking class—extra knightly points if you do!

Chapter Ten

FLOWERS, GIFTS, AND OTHER KNIGHTLY GESTURES

Although this has probably received adequate coverage elsewhere in this book, the subject of flowers, gifts, and other knightly gestures is important enough to merit its own brief chapter. It is just too easy for even a seasoned knight to "fall asleep at his post" and neglect a prime opportunity for a gesture that could add to the good pleasure and stability of his castle. Should you find that this has happened, just *get back on your horse* and slay the dragon of complacency with a creative flourish of an immediate kind.

THE TRUE MEANING OF FLOWERS AND GIFTS

Every man that "has the good sense God gave a goose" understands the importance of sending flowers to a lady, and, in particular, appreciates the deeper meaning of *roses*.

The first cultivated roses were reportedly grown in Asia over five thousand years ago—something that even your lady might not know. However, very few men truly comprehend the unique meaning behind the various colors of roses. Please permit me to provide the following primer on roses and to note the significance of color:

- Red Roses: True Love and Respect
- Red Rose Buds: Pure/Purity
- Rose Buds: Beauty, Youth, Innocence
- Red and White Roses: Unity
- Deep Burgundy Roses: Unconscious Beauty
- Bridal-White Roses: A Happy Love
- White Roses: Innocence, Purity, Secrecy
- White Rose Buds: Girlhood or Innocence
- Withered White Roses: Fleeting Beauty
- Yellow Roses: Joy, Friendship
- Pale Roses: Friendship
- Pink Roses: Grace
- Light Pink Roses: Sympathy
- Deep Pink Roses: Gratitude or Appreciation
- Coral or Orange Roses: Desire or Passion

The knight who knows his rose colors and their meanings is miles ahead of those vassals out there who wouldn't know one rose from another—let alone a flower's meaning and significance. Keep in mind that the knight knows these rose colors and their significance because his lady knows them. That's all you need to know, and you certainly don't want to infer a lack of chivalrous knowledge by sending the wrong color or the wrong message.

The timing of flowers can be important, as well, and flowers are expected on predictable dates, such as on Valentine's Day, birthdays, on anniversaries, and so forth. However, roses are most remembered and treasured when sent at no special time and merely as a confirmation of love or a reminder to your lady that, no matter where you are or what you are busy doing, she is often on your mind. These flowers will cheerfully adorn the spaces you share and be a constant reminder of the commitment and treasure of your mutual love. And, don't expect "paybacks." Her pleasure in receiving will be matched by your pleasure in giving beauty and happiness to another.

The best rule in sending flowers is to have no rule. Send them whenever you feel the urge to tell your lady that you love her and that she means everything to you! Each time you do, your love becomes stronger, your happiness with one another deeper and more enduring. Flowers are more than worth the time and expenditure you make to send them.

OTHER MEANINGFUL GESTURES

There are many other meaningful gestures that can reinforce your love for your lady and reaffirm your status as a knight-in-good-standing! The following are but a few of the many ways that you can remind her of your love, while reaffirming your love and commitment to your lady:

- Greeting cards (Hallmark® cards, etc.; especially those not tied to a particular date or event).

- A handwritten love letter (rare these days . . . and especially prized!)

- A personal poem of love (whether you're a poet or not, you'll be perceived as one by your lady!)

- Candy and a card (just to say "I love you").

- A gift certificate to an all-day spa (a special treat just for her).

- A prepaid weekend getaway for the two of you (or for her and a girlfriend).

- A special gift she has always wanted (and would never expect now).

- An e-mail just saying, "I love you!" (more on e-mails in the section that follows).

- Calling to tell her you have tickets to something she's been really wanting to see.

- Taking care of routine chores or responsibilities, thus giving her a free "me-day!"

- Anything else you can think of! (Be creative, knights!)

The mark of a true knight is a man who can both surprise with his thoughtfulness and arouse the passion in his lady through his consistent, knightly behavior. The practice of making routine gestures of love is an important aspect of reinforcing your love for her and her meaning in your life. In the end, you get what you give, gentlemen.

THE DAILY E-MAIL OR PHONE CALL

You may assume that simply sending a brief e-mail to your lady or picking up the phone and telling her that you were thinking of her doesn't mean much. Oh, *oblivious vassals are we!* What may seem very petty and unimportant to many men may be perceived as the manna of life by our ladies and be just the *shot in the arm* or pick-me-up they need to make their day brighter!

You may have been on her mind all the day long, and just hearing from you that you felt the same way reinforces that there is truly a connection between you, that things are good. Again, your lady, no matter whether she already knows deep down inside that you *do* truly love her, needs the regular reassurance and reinforcement that these daily contacts provide. It doesn't have to be a lengthy call or e-mail, unless you have the time for it and a great deal to say. That's wonderful, too. However, just a short note to tell her that you thought of her today—and that may be all she needs. Make these small contacts a daily part of your routine, all of your life, and you will qualify as an exceptionally chivalrous knight!

❦Sending Greeting Cards

While sending cards for anniversaries, birthdays, and other events is an essential part of every woman's life and routine, very few men are acclimated to the practice of sending cards just to re-affirm their love or share their thoughts with their lady. However, the knight who can make card-sending even a periodic part of his knightly behaviors will make a statement rarely seen even among the best First Knights, displaying behavior that will be envied by other knights!

Again, send cards for no reason, and send them often, but not *too* often! You wouldn't want to spoil your lady by overdoing it! (*Smile*).

Chapter Eleven

THE "SIZE OF A MAN'S HONOR"

"Size is everything," as they may say, and it's very true. The size of a man's character and the impact that his character has upon his stature as both a man of honor and as a chivalrous knight is all-important in how he is perceived and respected by the lady in his life, by his family and friends, and by the society of which he is an indispensable part.

WHAT IS KNIGHTLY STATURE?

Knightly stature is the demeanor that accompanies today's knight in everything he says and does. It is exemplified through both his words and actions and defines who he is and the ideals and principles for which he stands. It can best be defined as "the lasting impression he leaves among those he has touched" in his daily life. Furthermore, it includes what his words and actions say about his life, about his convictions, and about the level of sincerity of the Christian ideals that form the foundation of his life. Simply put, knightly stature can best be described as the very *essence* of a Godly and chivalrous man and of who and what he really stands for, as evidenced by his actual deeds, observed and recorded, in his everyday life.

Knightly stature is best reflected by a man of honor. But what is honor? More importantly, what has happened to the principle of honor among us as a society? Most of us can readily identify a man who is less than honorable; i.e., someone who cheats, lies, is dishonest in his relationship, marriage, or business dealings. However, being *honorable* is more than merely possessing or exhibiting certain virtuous characteristics, but, is about an individual who makes the characteristics of honesty, fairness, equity among people, and truthfulness an inseparable component of his life—indistinguishable from himself.

It is innate within the man of honor not merely to speak of these virtues but also to cherish them as essential to the quality life he strives ever to live and respect in regard to others. It is also indicative of a man who seeks the best for the society in which he and his family live and reflects his undying commitment to that society in order to ensure its preservation and perpetual prosperity. To the degree that those within a population exude honor, so is the society itself an honorable one. *How about yourself? Can you be counted as an honorable member?*

A perfect example of men of honor would be those U.S. and allied soldiers who fought in World War II, the Korean Conflict, the Viet Nam War, Desert Storm, and now, Operation Enduring Freedom. They are modern-day knights who have placed the security of their own country above their very lives. Included in this group of chivalrous knights are, also, the police and other law enforcement officers and firefighters who perished while doing their duty attempting to rescue those trapped in the World Trade Center and The Pentagon during the attacks on September 11, 2001. Lastly, but certainly not least, were those brave individuals, private citizens, who apparently attempted and successfully thwarted the fourth terrorist airline hijacking on 9.11.01, those who crashed in Pennsylvania and, according to reports, prevented an attack on some target in Washington, D.C., possibly The White House itself. These brave civilian heroes were men and women of knightly stature who set the standard of honor for all to recognize and follow.

Many proceed through life pretending to be honorable, much as people pretend to be Christians on Sunday then do whatever they wish, not honoring God, every other day of the week. Like our Christian walk and testimony, being honorable is not a part-time or one-day-per-week affair, but is the basis for our very lives. It is the way we *really* live, behave, and treat others, and that without pretense or aforethought. Those that perished on 9.11.01 did what they could to help others and were sterling examples of selfless honor, reminiscent of the knights of The Crusades. Why merely pretend to be honorable when we should be honorable as a matter of daily practice?

Knightly stature not only refers to honor but to the knightly standards we establish for ourselves in our daily lives and in our relationships with others, especially those close to us. *Do we treat others with courtesy and compassion, patience, empathy, respect, charity, Christian love, and selflessness?* Do we do everything possible to live our lives according to God's laws while supporting what is right and just and good in the society in which we live?

Today's knight learns from the "Code of Chivalry," established almost a thousand years ago with its tenets of Christian faith, respect for and protection of the weak, love of country, responsibility to family, honesty, and generosity—while at the same time fiercely opposing Satan and all that is evil around him—championing that which is right and good.

❧THE IMPORTANCE OF CHARACTER TO WOMEN

What does a man's character say about him? As a knight you will strive to be the epitome of virtue, honesty, and right character. Women seek a unique combination of toughness and gentility in a man. That is, most want a man who is gentle and caring, a man of integrity, compassion, honesty, sensitivity, openness, and stability. Yet, a woman also seeks a man of strength.

Society needs men of this mettle, as well! A woman—and *our world*, if you will—seeks a man who is both strong and approachable, a man who has the capacity for emotional intimacy, which we spoke of earlier, and the ability to make the tough decisions that are often necessary in the marketplace today or in today's society.

A man without such traits may be handsome, physically attractive, and highly desirable on the surface, yet he may lack substance. And just as an attractive woman can captivate a man for a short time, there must be more substance to a man than his physical attractiveness in order for an emotionally intimate and spiritual connection to form between he and his lady. When the inner qualities we've spoken of are there, however, a man offers much to his lady and adds quality to the world in which he lives.

While the physical attractiveness and beauty of men and women may well fade with time, our capacity, as men, for intimacy and our search for spiritual strength only intensifies as we become less ephemeral and mortal in our thinking and more focused on the immortal and eternal. People who attend church regularly and who have a personal relationship with Jesus Christ know this already. The goal of every true Christian, modern-day knight should be the empowerment of others to "think eternally, and not in mortal terms."

Going further, the knight who is truly in love will always look upon his lady as the most beautiful woman in the world, regardless of her age or time of life, and will always picture her in his mind as such and thus remind her, forever and a day, for all of his life, of her immense beauty in his eyes. A man of faith is a man who easily recognizes and readily acknowledges goodness and beauty, whether in a woman, or in the world around him, of which he is an essential part.

A woman both needs and wants a chivalrous man who knows who he is, what he wants, and where he is going. Just as importantly, he must show her how he intends to get there. But the *pursuit of goodness* is not just about money, although he must do his best to be fiscally responsible. As a woman gets older, it seems that her focus shifts somewhat to a greater interest in the man as an individual; in other words, what he is "inside"—his makeup, his true convictions, and where his priorities are in life, as opposed to merely "what he has." This takes a great deal of pressure off of the man as he can sense it and it has the potential to open the door to true intimacy.

While there are certainly "users" in both sexes who are focused only on what someone can do for them or give them; i.e., the "What have you done for me lately?" mentality (gold-diggers and players; there are lots of synonyms for them). As we grow older, many begin to realize that life is not about what we can "get" from one another, but what we can "share together" and *what makes us grow together* in God's eyes and what will prepare us for eternity. If we can reach this point, we have reached an epiphany of sorts, because we have made the transfer from a *mortal mentality* to one that is truly eternal in nature. Simply put, we're closer to God than ever before and have the hope of eternal life, if we will only commit ourselves to Christ. The chivalrous man recognizes this bridge and crosses it willingly.

It is this romantic abandon to our faith, our Christian commitment, or our "stepping out by faith," as we may call it, that really defines the character of a man whose focus is eternal as opposed to secular. It is this type of godly man who wishes to see that all around him seek and secure eternal life through exposure to God, His church Body, and the saving grace of Jesus Christ. The godly man and chivalrous knight whose focus is eternal is no longer a *user* in any sense of the word but a true giver, the right *kind* of giver—a witness *of* life and *for* life. If a man is a man of honor, it is second nature to him to treat all around him with love, grace, compassion, humility, generosity, respect, and a boundless giving of Christian charity.

What It Says About You

The quality of your character and how you actually live your daily life as a knight is a mirror of who you really are and what you are all about. While the *pretend knight* may fool some of the people some of the time, his wicked nature will ultimately be exposed, and others will see the vassal for what he actually is. Your *character* reveals your personality—including your thoughts and feelings on various matters, your priorities, and your strength as a person. A man of character and honor may bend under adversity, but, even so, he will never break, even in severe trials, but will emerge stronger, both physically, emotionally, and in his convictions—for they have proven their mettle in carrying him through the adversity from which he has emerged, victorious.

In the end, his trials are only tests from God, in many cases designed to build perseverance and character, promoting his spiritual growth. Truly God's knight of the twenty-first century, our man's Christian strength and conviction will shine brightly through dark valleys. Adversity only strengthens the Christian man, for it demonstrates that God is truly with him.

A knightly man of character knows that to be a true knight in principle is an arduous task, yet he accepts the challenge willingly with zeal and determination. Further, this knightly man continues to seek to know God more deeply and to expand his faith horizons through prayer, Bible study, and in his daily ministry toward others.

THE DEFINITION OF TRUE STRENGTH

The knightly man knows that the definition of "true strength" lies in his faith in God and in the Lord's principles, acknowledging that *all things* and *all strengths* come from God. Therefore, his efforts and his emphasis rest in God's character alone. The true knight is not deterred by failure or temporary distractions but shakes them off and redoubles his efforts to exhibit a character reflective of God's own on the pathway of righteousness and truth.

Chapter Twelve

AT ARM'S LENGTH— *BESIDE YOU*

While this chapter may not prove a particularly lengthy one, it unquestionably contains a concept of critical importance in our study—one that a knight must embrace and adopt as part of his everyday life if he is to be a *true chivalrous knight* in his lady's eyes. I trust that you will give it some thought and practice the model it promotes.

THE CONFLICT INHERENT IN MODERN ROLE DEFINITIONS

From our earliest training as men-to-be we are taught that our role as *protector* should be that of a man who runs his home as his castle—with an iron hand and with *total control*—one whose word and decisions are never questioned. While that concept may have worked in another era (and although there is something to be said for a man who is decisive at the right moment), times have changed, gentlemen, and so must we.

The twenty-first century is a new millennium with a new global environment and with new rules. That is not to say that we as men should compromise our Christian beliefs or our charge to show leadership in our homes. However, it does suggest that we can strengthen our homes by exercising sensitivity and discretion in a new, subtle but still powerful, way.

Like men, women have been "trained" by their mothers (and, maybe, their fathers, as well) to expect a man to be a certain type of person, one who possess assumed characteristics, in order to qualify as a "real man." In other words, there is supposed to be a *template* somewhere that defines the "ideal man" as macho, tough, decisive, manly, stoic, etc., and society's work is to squeeze every young male child into it, often at the loss of his true self. I've always wondered where this "ideal man" ideology came from, and more importantly, how it can be expected to survive. *What's the problem?* It seems there is a built-in conflict of intentions between men and women that can make for fireworks at every level.

Today's woman wants and expects a unique dynamic—total freedom and free rein to do whatever she wants, whenever she wants, without compromise to her freedom and with the ability to change her mind or direction on a dime. In short, the template of "what a man is supposed to be" may no longer fit with this "new woman," hence the conflicts between the two. Men are expected not only to understand what women want but to have the complete inventory of perceptual skills and flexibility to immediately recognize any change in plans and to adjust accordingly. This is no easy trick, ladies! Now let's think about it: how can a man be "Johnny-on-the-spot" the minute he's needed, ready to respond with the proper actions, when he has been provided no time to understand the *whys* and the *wherefores*—then, make sure he's nowhere to be seen when his presence isn't required.

Men just aren't programmed that way! It doesn't mean that we are dumb or insensitive; it merely reflects our inability to read minds. My point is this. The template of the "ideal man," whatever *that* may be, of a man who is the undisputed leader of his castle with unbending rod and rule, will almost assuredly clash with the lady who defers to no man.

Our modern society has become one in which men's and women's roles have become blurred, to say the least. Many men are not sure *what* their role is anymore. Further, men who are trapped in the obsolete philosophies of who and what a man "should be" are simply lost in a sandstorm with an outdated map, and will most certainly clash with today's lady when she is predisposed to *having it all.* Clearly, consideration of the other is needed on both ends.

❧The Art of "Being There, But Just Out of the Way"

Today's knight is the modern-day equivalent of a Renaissance Man. Not only is he balanced, perceptive, and grounded in the finer things of life, but he is trying to live the best Christian life he can. He balances his lady's need for independence and autonomy—making himself easily accessible but unobtrusive. He carries himself with a demeanor that is not the least bit threatened at the "tightrope" he walks. This is a feat that relatively few men have ever mastered, which would explain the fifty percent divorce rate we see in our country today.

Aside from the financial pressures that account for a great deal of the marital problems and divorces seen today (which occur less frequently in Christ-centered homes, but do also occur there), much conflict may be stemming from 1) the rapidly changing roles of men and women, 2) the couple's inability to perceive these changes or to quickly adjust to them, and, 3) their impatience and intolerance for the fact that their partner may not immediately comprehend or readily anticipate what they really want, yet do little or nothing to help each other understand their needs.

Put simply, mastering the art of "being there, but just out of the way" requires a very strong, secure man—and the total commitment of today's knight. It involves the realization that no matter how Christ-centered your home may be or how intimate your relationship with one another is, your lady may want and need her own life and identity, her career, and friendships with others. The man that can stand "a few feet to the side, just out of reach," yet lovingly enjoy his wife and encourage her to be who she is and who she needs to be while still remaining close enough to be there for her, is an exceptionally strong man.

Let me make something very clear and provide the following caveat: there is an inherent danger in doing this too freely, as temptation everywhere abounds, and the woman who abuses the freedom her knight provides her can open herself up to temptations that may jeopardize or even destroy their marriage. She, like her knight, however, must be equally committed to the marriage in order for it to work. A Christ-centered marriage is an equal opportunity relationship characterized by a close, personal, intimate relationship between husband and wife. In this scenario, the relationship will not only survive, but also will prosper, so long as both understand and agree to what degree of *separateness* and *connectedness* is safe and what poses a threat. However, the Christian man must step out in faith here sometimes, as well. As a knight he is honor-bound to protect the integrity of his home, and he should be prepared to speak his mind if he feels that the marriage is being strained by either too much or too little close contact.

Today's knight loves his lady enough to be right there if needed—but not *hovering*. He allows his lady the freedom to grow and be herself, something some of us are too insecure to permit. It may take awhile to realize that the man who attempts to restrain or overly confine the lady in his life in her daily activities runs the obvious risk of losing her, anyway. I have tried to practice "allowance of space" in my relationships, and *yes*, there have been times that it has been abused. However, some of those relationships were also not God-centered relationships, so they were doomed from the beginning, anyway. I believe that the man who enjoys a Christ-centered marriage, who stays just out of reach and doesn't interfere, but who can be there for his wife when needed or wanted, will be a knight that enjoys a wonderful, intimate, Christian-centered marriage.

One qualifier here: the knight, while making the commitment to stay "at arm's length but close by, if needed," has both the right and the obligation to protect his marriage from all threats and will take the steps necessary to discuss any concerns he may have with his lady so as to ensure the integrity of their marriage.

❧Respecting Her Right to Be Herself

The knight must respect the fact that his wife is also an individual with her own feelings, needs, wants, desires, friendships, and dreams. It takes a man who not only truly loves his lady but who also *respects* her deeply to stand aside while she "shines in her own light"—whether in her work and career, in her personal friendships, in family relationships, or in other ways. Not to do so would limit her potential, creating resentment and eventual problems in the relationship. Further, a man who not only understands his wife but openly supports her life and her dreams and ambitions is a man that she'll not only embrace, but grow ever more deeply in love with day by day.

It must be stressed here that this scenario has little probability of occurring unless the relationship is built on a strong Christian foundation, with both husband and wife totally committed to their marriage and in total agreement as to what constitutes healthy interpersonal behavior and what does not. Cultivating your beliefs and values as a couple (i.e., establishing, communicating, and reiterating them often together) is the equal responsibility of both the man and woman/ husband and wife, not just the knight.

❧*Needing You*, versus *Wanting You There*

Your lady will certainly *need* you at times, while at other times, she may not need you but may *want* you by her side. She may hesitate to admit to you that she needs you, as many women find it difficult to admit that they actually need the strength and reassurance of the man in their lives. However, and to be fair, men, while we can readily admit that we *want* or *desire* a woman, we are just as hesitant to admit that we actually *need* a woman, since it may make us appear weak or less of a man, either to her or to others. If we could just cut through the pretense, we would find that, truth be told, we both need and want each other at one time or another, and it's perfectly OK that we do. The concept of "needing you, versus wanting you there" also lends itself to the principles discussed in the preceding paragraphs; i.e., the artful practice of being there as men, but being "just out of the way, yet close by" when our lady needs or wants us. It's a balancing act, to be sure, but one that is well within the capabilities of the true chivalrous knight.

It's a very difficult thing for a man to "stand apart" from his lady when everything in his being says flatly that he needs to be right there. It's just how we men were made. Guardianship is ingrained deeply within us. It's the protector in us, I suppose, that wants to "stand guard over our lady," while in truth it may also involve a bit of closet insecurity. The fact is, you should be right there, but not in a smothering or *hovering* type of way. Don't make the mistake of trying to dictate her life and her daily routine. A knight is far more astute than that! Rather, you should openly respect and allow for her friendships and relationships, even with members of the opposite sex, even when you don't quite understand them or think that they even make sense. In short, prize her, and realize that, as the prize that she is, she is a treasure for the world to share—that you are God's steward of her as one of his greatest gifts! Thus you will demonstrate the strength of a godly man, secure in love and in a companionship relationship that is Christ-centered.

KNIGHTS: DON'T HOVER

One simple tenet here, knights of the twenty-first century: *hovering* is not cool. Be close by, if needed, but show your love and that you're secure in your relationship by giving her ladyship the *space* and place she deserves.

Chapter Thirteen

THE KNIGHTLY CHRISTIAN MAN

Preceding chapters have been dedicated to characteristics and behaviors that best define the chivalrous knight. While today's true knight is many things—*kind, generous, compassionate, caring, a man who is passionate about his lady's and his family's well-being, a man who expresses and acts upon his deep love of country and is willing to defend it*—the true chivalrous knight is almost certainly a God-fearing man.

⚑ TWO TYPES OF MEN

There seem to be two types of men today: those who think "above the waist" and those who think "below the waist." Men who think *below* the waist could best be described as men of Epicurean taste, those who live for today and all of life's momentary and secular pleasures. These men are preoccupied with procuring material things and having a good time which typically includes a predominant preoccupation with immediate and frequent sexual fulfillment without commitment. In short, men who think below the waist are essentially interested in their own personal, sexual pleasure and gratification. They are in no way interested in a permanent relationship with a woman—much less a true lady. While some men lie about their feelings or intentions in order to get what they want, others are blatantly honest about their lack of commitment and their true intentions. Whatever the approach, there are more than enough women who *also* think below the waist (or who simply don't care) to accommodate them.

Common terms for these men include: "players," "users," "jerks," and stronger names which will be left to the imagination. In short, such men use women for their own convenience or for whatever sexual pleasure or satisfaction they can obtain with absolutely no stirring of conscience or remorse. Unfortunately, these men leave a trail of emotional destruction in their wake, creating the incorrect perception among many women that, "All men are jerks."

Even more tragic is the fact that men who think below the waist and who behave in this way have done as much damage to themselves, because a little bit of who they really are or *could be* gets buried with every abusive relationship. With each relationship they become a bit more hardened in their behavior and a bit less capable of feeling and achieving true intimacy with a woman. In short, the unfeeling man becomes less and less able to feel and moves ever closer to living a life alone without feelings, intimacy, or the ability to truly love another—to a *living death,* or precisely what Satan would like to inflict upon us all! If the devil can numb our senses, feelings, and ability to truly love another in a deeply committed marital relationship, is he not closer to achieving his eternal goal of numbing our souls and separating us from God for all eternity?

Conversely, men who think "above the waist" are generally intelligent, thinking, caring, passionate, thoughtful men of culture, exhibiting social and emotional finesse. Men who earn the designation of belonging to this group readily recognize the preciousness of the wondrous gift God has provided in the form of their lady. They strive to do everything in their power to treat all women with courtesy, respect, caring, compassion, and Christian reverence. Men who think and live their lives *above the waist* have usually experienced an epiphany at some time in their lives. They want to truly live and love. They want to appreciate all that God's creation has to offer—the richness of the arts, the beauty of the world around them, a life of honor and Christian charity, a family and an intimate relationship that leads to a Christ-centered marriage.

Through their epiphany they have recognized the sinfulness of *using* others (men and women alike) and begun striving to love and appreciate others. At some point in our lives, if we are fortunate enough, some key insight reaches us. It's the point at which we have grown beyond the adolescent fantasies which continue to drive the behavior of the first group. If we are successful in reaching this position in our lives, our focus as men shifts from those things that are "temporal" or secular to those things that are truly imperishable. It's tough and brutal for a man to finally realize that he has been living his life in a sinful, wasteful, unproductive and non-spiritual manner, as is so often the case with those men who *think below the waist.*

Men who think *above* the waist are thinking with the 'eternal' organs, the brain and heart, rather than the temporal one. Their connections aren't temporary but are permanent. Through divine revelation these men have come to appreciate that marriage is, in fact, God's way of ensuring that not only does man have a lifelong companion, but that marriage, a *good marriage,* is God's way of seeing to it that we, as men, focus on the eternal. A healthy marriage centered in Christ grounds the man by concentrating his thoughts, actions, and energies on the preparation of his soul for eternity. It also provides him a stable, safe, and loving environment cultivated by his lady, whereby his soul is both nurtured and protected from the numbing effect of the secular world around him. A good marriage does another thing for a man: it removes the constant preoccupation with sex by replacing it with a preoccupation with love and intimacy. However, this reduced obsession with sex, rather than diminishing the act, only amplifies the level of intimacy.

Marriage is designed to prepare the man for eternity while offering him a richer life through years of physical, emotional, and spiritual intimacy with a life-partner in the form of a loving woman, his *lady faire*.

❧THE KNIGHTLY CHRISTIAN MAN

What is the knightly Christian man? First let's examine what makes a man a *knightly man*. So far we have identified just what makes a man a chivalrous knight; i.e., those principles and characteristics that exemplify a man of true class, honor, discretion, compassion, honesty, integrity, and dignity. The chivalrous knight cares about family and friends, has a deeply rooted love of country, and is ready and willing to defend it. He is a gentle, loving man, but also, is quick to act in defense of his lady or family, and is a selfless man who gives of himself, even when he has nothing to give. He is also a man who loves the arts and all the good and creative experiences that the world has to offer; he is overtly generous and charitable, and a man who knows how to treat and respect his lady, and how to express his love and adoration for her. *Can a man who exhibits such characteristics be a man who thinks below the waist?* I don't think so.

It's often said that, "Men think with their brains, while women think with their hearts." There *is* a lot of truth to that statement. Women often act upon their emotions, while men have been strictly disciplined to think with their brains and dismiss "feeling stuff." The challenge for some men, however, is to make a clear decision on, "Which brain do I think with?" The man who expresses chivalrous traits is a man who has made a concerted decision to think with the brain that is located *above* the waist. If a man thinks with this brain, he also thinks with another organ located north of his belt buckle: his heart.

If the knightly man thinks with both his brain *and* his heart, he has the potential to be closer to God and is in a much better position to seek and find Him, for he is not as far removed from Him as the "earthbound" Neanderthal Man. He has come to realize the value of life and has a far better ability and potential to visualize things from an eternal perspective as opposed to a temporal one. Consequently, the man who thinks *above the waist* and who thinks/feels with both his brain and his heart is in a far better position to understand God's plan for human life and for himself. The transition from merely displaying knightly stature to coming into the full stature of a knightly Christian man is a relatively simple one, given a sincere wish to find God and a pure heart with which to seek Him.

The knightly Christian man first seeks God in everything that he thinks, says, and does: the way he dresses, the way he treats and respects others and their feelings, his generosity and charity in everyday life and in support of the Church and its Mission, his demonstrated love and compassion for his lady and family, and his patriotism and concern for his country's preservation and continued prosperity. All of these identify and reinforce the man and *who he is* as a knight. If he is a true knight, he embraces and exemplifies all that the "Code of Chivalry" stands for including its three key tenets (see above), which are founded on Christian principles.

If the knight already lives his life according to these knightly guidelines, is he not infinitely closer to living the life of a Christian man, as well, as he seeks his God? The chivalrous knight already lives his faith-based convictions and wholesome beliefs in his daily life. A man who lives his life in such a decent and meaningful way is predisposed to find God, for he realizes that there is something far bigger and more important than himself. He already lives his life placing others ahead of himself. A man who places the needs of others ahead of his own is a mirror of Jesus, who placed the need of humanity for Salvation ahead of His own life, relinquishing self for us. Offering our lives in similar small, selfless ways, we inevitably find ourselves closer to God and are more capable of seeking—*and finding*—Him.

LIVING THE STRENGTH OF YOUR FAITH

Living the strength of your faith is the trademark of the knightly Christian Man. There is no mistaking this man, nor his sincere mission and his level of commitment to God, his lady, and his family.

This man is a man of balance and stability—emotionally, financially, and spiritually. This man, in recognizing and emphasizing the *eternal* versus the *temporal,* lives his life according to God and His laws and forsakes the fleeting offerings and temptations of the world. He is a man of honor, trust, integrity, sincerity, generosity, charity, love, compassion, and "quiet strength" . . . a secure man who can let others live and prosper to their true potential without fear or insecurity. He is a man who obeys the Bible when it says to, ". . . elevate your wife" and he shows her all of the love, respect, and adoration that he possibly can express to her. He reassures her continually that he loves her, that he wants and needs her, and he regularly and lovingly reminds her that she means everything to him. He also lives his life according to the "Code of Chivalry," without compromise, giving selflessly to others, treating everyone alike and in the respectful manner that God intended for us to treat others.

Characteristics of the Knightly Christian Man

Living the strength of his faith with honor, we can say of the knight that:

- He is a man who loves his wife or lady, and who professes it proudly.

- He is a man who cherishes his children, whose priority is in teaching what is "right and good" to them.

- He is a man who honors his father and mother, as God commanded.

- He is a man who lives his life according to the Ten Commandments as best he can.

- He is a man who is prepared to meet God, and who is both assured of and secure in his Salvation.

- He is a man who abides by the "Code of Chivalry" and its tenets.

- He is a man of outreach, who attends church regularly and supports its mission with his time, talents, and financial resources.

- He is a man of compassion who eagerly helps others—his lady, family, friends, the underprivileged—in any way he can without complaint or hesitation.

- He is a man who loves his country and works diligently in his own way to contribute to its prosperity.

- He is a man of conviction who will defend his country against "infidels."

- He is a man who lives a life of honesty and integrity.

- He is a man of *finesse*, a diplomat who acts selflessly while elevating others.

- He is a man of discretion who holds his tongue while sparing others' feelings.

- He is a man who is not afraid to share his innermost intimate feelings with his wife or lady.

- He is a man who seeks emotional, physical, and spiritual intimacy with his wife or lady.

- He is a man who continually seeks his God, and inquires of His will for his life.

- He is a man who focuses on the *eternal* versus the *temporal*.

- He is a man of *faith* and literacy who reads the Bible.

- He is a man of *speech and thought* who prays regularly.

- He is a man of *action* who serves God in his daily life.

- He is a man who *believes* without having seen and believes in Jesus Christ.

- He is a man of *love* who seeks to love those around him.

- He is a man of *quiet strength* who is there, just out of reach, but present if needed.

- He is a man of justice, goodness, and rightness in all things.

Again, the true Christian knight cannot be confused with other men—he is outstanding, envied, and an example for all around him—a true honor to those knights of a thousand years ago who would look upon him today and be pleased by his exemplification of *right* and *good*.

THE PRESENCE OF STRENGTH IN HUMILITY

Men are predisposed to think in terms of seeking success, yet in our being defined not as individuals but in terms of how "successful" we are, we have unwittingly become creatures of ego. I say this primarily because men are expected to be "successes," else they have no worth in the eyes of others, particularly the ladies we wish to impress most of all. Ego is the personification of our success, shouting, "Look at me; I'm a success." Unfortunately, often who we are as men is defined by society as "what we do" or "what we have" rather than "who and what we are." However, *humility*, a highly desirable attribute that would predispose us to godliness, is by necessity replaced by ego or *the absence of humility*. In other words, the pressure placed upon us by the world around us to be a success prevents us from being humble men of quiet strength. In fact, men who exhibit humility and the absence of ego are looked upon with some suspicion and may even be considered weak or undesirable.

The Christian chivalrous knight has learned a profound fact, however: there is great strength in humility. Else, why would Jesus have washed the feet of another? Was that not the ultimate act of humility? If Jesus, the Son of God, could exhibit such humility, could we not learn from that example, as well? A man who practices humility humbles himself before God. More profoundly, in doing so, he makes the statement that, "I humble myself, for I know that there is One infinitely greater than I; therefore, I am insignificant in His sight, and I humble myself before Him." Humility is, for that very reason, a profound profession of faith in God. The knight who expresses humility also expresses his faith, for he is not boastful, but humble, which elevates him before God.

Humility can be expressed in many ways, from elevating others while humbling oneself, to "turning the other cheek," as Jesus taught us to do. Or, it can consist of living life in a humble but secure way, serving others before oneself. The knight knows this and lives his life in the humble service of others.

❧ELEVATING YOUR LADY LOVE

The Christian man is especially careful to treat his lady with all of the love, adoration, courtesy, respect, dignity, and kindness that is possible, while always affirming his love and desire for her. As we've seen, *foreplay* is not only a sexual term, but is much broader and more meaningful in terms of stroking the affections and building the inner security of your lady. It should form the foundation for a way of life in which you elevate your lady, making her feel desired and reinforcing what you say so that she knows she is truly the only woman in the world for you. For if you are the Christian knight you claim to be, she is everything to you, and more. She is the love of your life and the lady of your life. Elevate her in everyday things—in everything you think, say, and do. Cherish her for what she is: your confidant, lover, and the life-partner that God in his infinite wisdom brought to you as part of His plan for blessing your life.

❧PUT CHRIST AT THE CENTER OF YOUR CASTLE: THE GODLY MARRIAGE

"A house divided against itself cannot stand" (Matt: 12:25). Why do so many marriages, over 50 percent now (according to the latest research in the U. S.) fail? Is it because the two persons involved simply don't take the time to get to know each other? Are poor financial planning decisions mainly to blame? Or, is it that they are just incompatible sexually, intellectually, or emotionally? Do they not like the same activities or aren't they as compatible as they originally thought they were? While these factors all certainly play *some* role in marital conflict, the absence of Christ working at the center and standing as the foundation of the marriage is the major factor. The following three points give reasons for the importance of a Christ-centered marriage:

1. The Foundation

   In not being Christ-centered, the marriage is not biblically-grounded. A marriage that is founded on the Bible and its teachings (including the Ten Commandments and Christ's own teachings) is a marriage that will grow and thrive from the richness of God's plan for each spouse's life, and in their common purpose as *one new being* in God's eyes; that is, the Salvation of both individuals and the assurance that each has that their life together and how they live their lives as individuals in partnership with one another will prepare both of them for eternity.

2. The Blueprint

   A marriage or a serious relationship, involving non-Christians where one or both of the partners are not actively seeking God's will creates a scenario in which one of them may seek something foreign or potentially destructive to their goals. How can, "A house divided against itself . . ." stand? While one spouse may endeavor to grow in his or her walk with God through fellowship with His Son, Jesus Christ, the other spouse, who may not be a Christian, may not appreciate the value or meaning of a personal relationship with Christ. Thus, the partner may not only be passively resistant to their partner's 'faith-goal', but may openly mock or even attempt to discourage the Christian partner from pursuing his or her faith, creating a serious dilemma and conflict. This marriage will not last and, may in fact, serve to damage or destroy the Christian's own efforts to follow God.

3. The Destination

A marriage not based in Christ is a marriage without a road map, driving directions, or a destination. Where do the two parties involved plan to go as a couple? What is their ultimate destination? *Why* are they going in that direction? How do they get there, together (prayer, love, church, God's Word, tithes and offerings)? The marriage that is absent of Christ is a body without a head—with no brain, no common purpose, no thought process, no plan, no thought—and with an absence of reason and eternal foresight. I now believe more than ever that God intended for marriage to be the foundation whereby two people could support, love, and assist each other's quest for God and move toward eternal Salvation while *being here* for each other in matters of safety, security, passion, and love. In short, our partner can be God's wonderful traveling companion, brought to us by Him, as we walk forward together, by God's grace, into eternity.

THE KNIGHTLY MAN IS A GODLY MAN

The knightly man is a godly man in all that he thinks, says, and does—and in everything he believes as a man. He is a sincere, moral man who actively seeks God and the *good* and *right* in everything: in the people he meets, as well as, with his family. However, he is not in any way deluded into believing that the Evil One is not real and does not exist. Consequently, he is a man of dutiful vigilance ever-endeavoring to protect his home, his lady, his family, and his country against the dangerous attacks of the Evil One. The knightly Christian man wants to ensure that his home is Christ-centered, for he loves his lady and his family and cares deeply for their own Salvation so that *they* receive the gift of eternal life through God's grace. Hence, he will do his utmost to create a home environment that is not merely chivalrous, but moral and Christian—a home exemplified by love, honor, caring, and compassion, with all living within God's laws. He will live his life as an example to his family and to others. His home is centered on Jesus Christ and, as such, is richly blessed—a house that cannot be divided. The godly man wants a godly marriage because in his wisdom he knows that having any other kind is folly.

Chapter Fourteen

CHIVALROUS BEHAVIORS AND THE BIBLE

Throughout this book, we have discussed many attributes of the chivalrous man and of those noble characteristics which should differentiate him from other men who may believe, behave, and live in a manner that is less than chivalrous. It has been inferred widely throughout the pages of this book as well that, in order to live the life of a true chivalrous knight, it is essential that our knight live his life according to Christian principles. The intent of this chapter is to provide an introduction to those Biblical scriptures which support the walk of the Knightly Christian Man, so that he may know that his behaviors are not only based upon honor and integrity, but are of God and His Law.

SUPPORTING SCRIPTURES

A wealth of Biblical scripture supports the principles which guide the daily life of the chivalrous knight; however, for purposes of this book, we will offer only a number of introductory references in the hope of reinforcing the fact that much of those most desirable traits of the chivalrous man are also part of God's Commandments for our lives, and in many cases, from Jesus' own teachings. The key chivalrous principles of faith, honor, integrity, charity, selflessness, and other key traits so critical if we are to live chivalrous lives are categorized below and supported by scripture.

A. Faith

Faith is the substance of those things hoped for, yet unseen (Hebrews, 11:1); Faith is a work, and without faith, we cannot perform the works of God (Hebrews; James 2:14). Further, Faith comes from hearing (through listening), and hearing comes from God's Word (shall we not make listening a priority in all things?) (Romans 10:17);

If we are faithful, we will be obedient to God's Holy Word (Romans 1:5; Romans 10:17, and Romans 16:26);

Faith works through love, and we must have a 'living faith'. Further, we must act on faith by being 'doers' (James 1:21 through 1:27; Hebrews 4:2);

Further, we must feed our faith by virtue, for from virtue comes knowledge, and from knowledge comes self-control and restraint, from self-control, perseverance, and from perseverance, Godliness, and from Godliness, brotherly love and kindness, and thus, comes love for one another and for God (2 Peter 1: 5 through 11); and finally,

Faith is a part of God's gift of armor which He supplies to us to help us defend ourselves against the Devil and his attempts to distract us from our Knightly Mission of Christian service (Ephesians 6:11 through 18 and 1 Thessalonians 5: 6 through 28).

We as Chivalrous Christian Knights have been justified by our faith and are able to receive God's Grace through Jesus Christ by our faith in Him (Romans 5:1 through 2);

And, lastly, we are obedient to the faith (i.e., our faith in God and the unseen) (Romans 1:5 and Romans 16:26);

Being men of faith in Christ, we are well-rooted in his Will and built up for his service, and thus, are complete in Him (Colossians 2: 5 through 10)

B. Defense of Government and Authority

We must obey the governing authorities, as they are ap-
pointed by God Almighty. Further, The Lord God established
governments in order that evildoers would be punished, and
for the recognition of those that perform good deeds. Government is God's administrator in exercising justice upon those
who would do wrong, and, if we resist government, we also
resist God's ordinance (Romans 13:1 through 8 and 1 Peter
2:13 through 15).

We must obey the government for both the Lord's sake and
for the sake of conscience (Romans 13: 1 through 8).

C. Strength Through Humility, Wisdom, and Service to
Others

We derive strength through humility, wisdom, charity, honesty,
love, and selflessness. These principles of the chivalrous knight are
also supported through Biblical scripture:

We love without hypocrisy, and abhor evil, while clinging to what
is just and good, are kind and affectionate with others, and are
warriors in spirit as we serve our Lord. Further, we rejoice in
hope, and are patient in trials and tribulations, as we are steadfast
in the (exercise of) prayer (Romans 12: 9 through 12);

In humility, we present our bodies as living sacrifices to God
and man, being transformed through the renewal of ourselves
through knowledge (Romans 12: 1 through 2 and Colossians
3:1 through 16).

In humility, we associate with the humble, while remaining
humble in ourselves and our behaviors (Romans 12:2 through
21 and Philippians 2:1 through 4).

We live in peace with others as much as possible and love our
fellow man (Romans 12:18 and Romans 13: 8 through 10);

Our conduct is honorable, and worthy of the gospel of Jesus
Christ (1 Peter 2: 11 through 12 and Philippians 1:27);

We are sober and vigilant, careful not to deter from our steadfast mission of growing in the service of the Lord (1 Peter 5: 8 through 9 and 2 Peter 3:17 through 18);

On wisdom, our wisdom comes not from human sources or influences, but from the search for truth which comes only from God (1 Corinthians 3:18 through 23 and James 3:13 through 18). Further, as wise men, we walk 'in love', we walk 'in the light', and we walk 'in wisdom' through our walk with the Lord (Ephesians 5:1 through 21);

(As wise men with wisdom gained through our walk with God), we find ourselves ever closer towards the goal of Eternal Life. We have fellowship with God and walk in the light (Philippians 3:12 through 16 and 1 John 1:6 through 7).

As wise men, we maintain God's Commandments because of our love for Him, and because of our love, we do not fear His judgment (1 John, Chapters 2 through 5);

As wise men, we know that we must obey the Word of God, that God's Word is Truth, and that we must practice the truth in our daily lives (2 Thessalonians 2:1 through 17).

As wise men, God's peace protects both our hearts and minds through our prayers, as we follow the example of the apostles, for we are fulfilled through the richness of prayer. And as wise men, we dwell on those things which are noble, just, good, true, pure, and worthy of the love of God (Philippians 4:6 through 9);

As wise men who seek God through his Son Jesus Christ, we seek those things which are Eternal rather than of man, and set our minds on the things of God (Colossians 3: 1 through 2);

As wise men, we strive to lead a quiet, peaceful life within Christ, minding our own affairs, and accomplishing God's Work through our own labors, walking in God's Will and obeying the Word of God (1 Thessalonians 4:11 through 12 and 2 Thessalonians 3:1 through 18).

As wise men, we flee from Evil and pursue God's Righteousness, standing as warriors of faith with the fervent belief of Eternal life (1 Timothy 6: 1 through 12).

As wise men, we live by faith (not by sight), and become teachers, that others may know the Lord (Hebrews 5:12 through 14 and Hebrews 10:26); Blessed are those who have not seen and have believed (John 20:29).

As wise men, we pray for wisdom, asking for wisdom through faith (James 1: 5–8 and 5:15);

As wise men, we know, too, that obedience as Christian men comes from the heart and that we must obey God before man (Romans 6:17 and Acts, Chapters 4 and 5);

As patient men, we learn to live in peace and patience through whatever adversity life may present to us. We restrain our tongues, do not judge, do not prejudge, are humble, are friends with God, and do not boast, but have 'an obedient, living faith', living the Word of God. Further, we pray in earnest when we suffer, and sing when happy and joyful. We openly confess our trespasses to each other (Philippians 4:1 through 13 and James, Chapters 1-5).

On Christian pride, we are not ashamed, but boldly proclaim the Word of God and the gospel of Jesus Christ (Romans 1:16) (2 Timothy 1:8 and 1 Corinthians 1:18);

On Christian charity and selflessness, we are to serve the needs of the less fortunate, including other Christians, and are cheerful givers as the Lord has taught us (2 Corinthians 8:1 through 15 and 9:5 through 15).

Further, on selflessness, we bear others' burdens and thus fulfill Christ's instruction to us. Further, we do not grow tired or weary in doing good for others (Galatians 6:2 and 9 through 10);

In charity and on the topic of tithing and offerings, the Bible teaches us as chivalrous knights to financially support the spreading of the gospel of Jesus Christ (Galatians 6:9 through 10).

As loving men and chivalrous knights, we are to exhibit the characteristics of tenderness, kindness, humility, meekness, long suffering, and shining examples of charity, love, and forgiveness, as God's peace and love is foremost in our hearts and dwells richly through us. Further, our words and speech are gracious and kind (Colossians 3: 12 through 16 and 4:5 through 6).

As loving partners and husbands, we are to act properly with love and understanding towards our ladies and wives, else our prayers may not be honored (1 Peter, Chapter 3);

A man is as he thinks in his heart. Evil corrupts good morals, and, if our companions are Evil, our morals will be Evil also (Proverbs 23:7)

D. Men as Loving Husbands

Finally, the Bible also speaks of God's expectations for us as men in our relationships with our wives; that is, the commandment that "Husbands, love your wives just as Christ loved the church and gave himself up for her to make her holy, cleansing her by the washing with water throughout the word." Our directive as husbands continues in the next few verses, "In the same way, husbands ought to love their wives as their own bodies. He who loves his wife loves himself." (Ephesians Chapter 5). Thus, our Mission of service to our wives and the 'loves of our lives' if we are not yet married is spelled out very clearly in God's Holy Word. We are to both love, honor, cherish, and serve our wives, while loving them as we love ourselves. This is one of God's Holy ordinances.

THE ARMOR OF GOD

Much as the knights of The Crusades adorned their armor as protection before battle, it is equally essential that we as men adorn the Armor of God in order that we may carry out the good fight, both as chivalrous knights and as the Godly men we aspire to be. We must surround ourselves with God's full armor—His Commandments, God's Holy Word, and the powerful ally of Prayer as a combined, formidable weapon, coupled with a sincere, committed daily walk of faith. God's armor also includes the attributes of a godly man and chivalrous knight—truth, honesty, integrity, humility, selflessness, peace, patience, love, generosity and charity, and faith in a God in whom we believe, yet have never seen. It is hoped that the above biblical references not only support the principles outlined throughout this book, but give strength, reassurance and peace to all men, chivalrous knights or those who would-be chivalrous knights, for we all can benefit from their words.

Chapter Fifteen

In Closing: Knightly Knowledge

For those men who are still with me, you have gotten started on the pathway of chivalry already and may now be wondering, "How can I be a better knight"? Well, one of the best things the fledgling vassal can do to help him become a better man and a more chivalrous knight is to make a "knightly checklist."

The *checklist* may best be described as an "actual versus goal" target practice strategy. To begin with, make a list of those activities that you do right now, right or wrong, and then compare them against some of the suggestions made in this book. One of the best techniques I've found is to take out a sheet of paper and draw two columns across the top of the page, then draw a line down the center. At the top of the left-hand column write the words "The Ideal Knight: My Goals," and, on the right side, the words, "My Actual Knightly Actions."

Then, complete the "Ideal Knight" left-hand column *first* from those points in the book that you would like to incorporate into your own daily lifestyle. Once you have completed your column listing the ideals, you will strive to achieve, go ahead and complete the right-hand column with how you actually feel you "stack up" against the ideal knight in the various categories you've identified.

Once you complete both columns, you'll have a realistic view of what you *do well* as a knight, as well as what you could improve upon, thus elevating your status as a chivalrous knight.

When establishing goals for yourself, be sure not to set your short-term objectives too high, but plan to progress at a realistic pace so that you will have a good possibility of reaching your early improvement goals. Then, resume your efforts with a second set of short-term goals and, afterwards, repeat the process. Before you know it you'll be noticing dramatic improvement in your knightly skills and experiencing their daily impact upon your life, as well as your walk of faith. Best of all, your lady will also notice the change and appreciate you even more for your efforts to become a better, more well-rounded knight. Suddenly, you're the most essential man in her life!

PRACTICE MAKES PERFECT

The regular practice of many of these principles and suggestions will almost certainly help the would-be knight to be a more responsive partner to his lady—as well as, a better parent, spouse, and a more valuable member of his community and country. Practice those activities and suggestions outlined in the book that you feel will make you a better, more sensitive and responsive man, and it will very likely improve your life and relationship in many ways. Practice *does* make perfect, especially as it relates to improving our attitudes and behavior among others, particularly in the relationships with the women we love and cherish.

RELAX . . . AND ENJOY YOUR LIFE!

Frankly, incorporating the principles outlined in the chapters you've just read will not only improve your relationship with the lady of your life, but likely may improve your ability to enjoy your life and the things around you more completely! Relax, try the techniques and principles here and see if it makes a positive difference in your life. I am confident that it will. *Good luck, and May God Be With You Throughout This Process!*

ꟻConclusion

I hope that the men (and the ladies, too!) who have taken the time to read this book on chivalry have benefited from the thoughts and suggestions outlined herein. I have always felt that there was a close correlation between the "Code of Chivalry" and a man's Christian walk. In this post-September 11, 2001, world in which we now live, it's vitally important that each of us re-examine our life and introspect on how our lives are being lived.

Are we living our lives according to God's will? If we were to face our own 9.11 fate tomorrow, would we be prepared for eternity? Many who were trapped in the World Trade Center towers and in the Pentagon may not have been, nor were some of those who died in Pennsylvania. Little did they know how short their time would be to get right with God!

If you ask yourself, "What would my eternity have been had I been one of the victims on 9.11," what would your answer be? All pretenses aside, you know the answer. We all do, deep down inside. My answer would be that I would be in heaven now. There's no question that I am saved by grace because I have put my faith in Jesus Christ. If you're not ready, you know it, so why not speak with a pastor or a Christian friend about Jesus and what provision needs to be made for your eternal soul? In the course of encouraging knightly, Christian behavior among men, my hope and intent has been that it will help enlighten readers as to the true value and meaning of human life. I believe that as we come closer to chivalrous behavior, we come closer to God and to our own Salvation. The pursuit of chivalry did that for me, and it can perform the same wondrous miracle in your life, too.

A man who carries himself with class, discretion, and purpose is a man who will inevitably question his own life's direction at times, and one who is far more likely to arrive at the independent conclusion that there is much more to life than what we were taught to believe as teenagers. Our time in this life is about getting prepared for the *real* life to come, and the choice is ours alone. *Do we want an eternity with God, or do we choose eternity without Him?*

Simple question, and yet one that most of us de-emphasize or simply regard as insignificant. Gentlemen (and ladies reading this), there is nothing insignificant about where you will spend eternity; it's beyond our comprehension in significance. As men, if we become truly wise at some time in our lives, we begin to learn the critical lesson—that of the necessity of focusing strictly upon eternal issues. I have always loved Albert Einstein's quote, "I want to know God's thoughts. The rest are mere details." While certainly a genius, Einstein was a genius (in my view) in a far more profound way for which he probably was never recognized. He was apparently a very spiritually-wise man in yet another sense: in that he obviously understood the Presence and Majesty of God and the wisdom of thinking *eternally* versus *temporally.*

It's quite simply the most important lesson we can learn in life; that is, the eternal importance of seeking God and His will for our life. Recognizing this fact is second only in importance to becoming saved for all eternity through God's grace. Our belief that Jesus is the Son of God and placing our trust in Him for our future through baptism enables us to receive His gift.

As men, as Christian men, and as leaders of our castles, we can all take Einstein's words to heart and focus our thinking in just the same way. As men, let us search and seek God's thoughts and plans for our own lives, for all else is frivolous and utter folly. A billion years from now, when some man is burning in eternal torment, will he remember why he focused his life and time on buying things? *What will these things mean to him then? Could you be that man? What regrets may you have?* Now is the moment of opportunity, the time to change the direction of your life—not only in terms of chivalrous behavior and being a better man, but as a chivalrous Christian man. In terms of your soul, *where do you stand with God right this minute?*

One final thought: living a life of knightly stature with honor, compassion, love, integrity, spiritual strength, and honesty . . . in fellowship with Jesus Christ through God's grace, will be the combination that will get you to the right place in eternity. Your pursuit of chivalry, then, may well be a portal to finding God and his plan for your life in the most meaningful way possible; and, as such, the doorway to eternal life for you, your lady, and those within your home.

Chivalry is truly not dead, gentlemen. Indeed, it lives on and can thrive, if we choose, through our intention to live as godly Christian men throughout our lives, thus also living as true Christian knights. Are you up to the challenge, as were the brave knights of The Crusades of long ago and as were those chivalrous law enforcement officers, firefighters and emergency services personnel—and all the other brave, latter-day knights who died on 9.11.01? Or, of all those brave men and women who have died in Iraq?

Good knight, have a great life! I leave you with this charge: live as the chivalrous Christian knight you desire to be! Keep the faith. Consider the Code of Chivalry. May God Bless You, and I trust to see you in God's Heaven one day!

"Winning the Heart of the Special Lady in My Life": An Eight-Week Men's Ministry Small Group Bible Study

Introduction

I trust that the preceding pages of *The Chivalrous Man* have been an inspiration in empowering each and every one of you to lead lives of chivalrous Christian knighthood to the very best of your ability. The following is a suggested outline for use of this book as part of your Men's Ministry small group or men's breakfast/Bible study classes, or wherever men meet to support and empower one another in godly goals.

The program is divided into eight weekly segments with a weekly reading assignment and weekly written homework project. Week eight brings you to a final assessment, along with each man's creation of his own personal plan for enhancing his daily life of Christian chivalry.

Through this eight-week course and the use of this text as a guidebook, we sincerely trust that this exercise in Christian chivalry and personal spiritual growth will lead you to new heights in your relationships with your wife, your special lady, and other precious ladies in your life—members of your family, friends, coworkers, and others. Most of all, I hope it will enhance your relationship with God Almighty. Please feel free to modify the program to fit the needs and time constraints of your group. I look forward to hearing of your increasing satisfaction with and success in living the tenets of Christian chivalry.

God Bless!

Gary D. Milby

SUGGESTED PROGRAM STUDY TIMETABLE
(EIGHT WEEKS)

Week	Reading/Assignments	Suggested Discussion Topics
Week 1	Chapters 1, 2 Assign reading for next week; ask men to notice their behaviors and compare them to the Code.	*How does the "Code of Chivalry" relate to our lives as Christian men today? Is it helpful? Is it relevant? Is Chivalry dead or alive in society today?*
Week 2	Chapters 3, 4 Plan #1: Homework Assignment for Week 3 *How Can I Improve?* Set 3 Goals that you will attempt to reach in the next 30 days.	*Am I a chivalrous man? How do I rate with chivalrous compliments and the social graces? How is my lady responding?*
Week 3	Chapters 5, 6, 7 Plan #2 Homework Assignment for Week 4: *How can I improve?* Set 3 new goals from these chapters that you will attempt to achieve in the next 60 days.	*Am I a well-dressed, well-read, Christian man? Bible? Other books? Do I practice the "24/7 foreplay" techniques to compliment my wife or my special lady? How do others say I treat them? How is my lady responding?*
Week 4	Chapters 8, 9, 10 Plan #3 Homework Assignment for Week 5: Incorporate 3 new chivalrous actions towards your wife/lady into your daily life in the next week. Report efforts/ successes to the group in a 5-minute summary next week.	*Do I have a "knight's mentality?" How so? Any deficiencies? What can I/we do to improve? How is my lady responding?*

Week 5	Chapter 11 Plan #4 Homework Assignment for Week 6: Plan 3 daily activities that you are going to implement this next week that will make you a more honorable man. Report back your successes to the group next week.	*Am I honorable as a Christian man? How can I be more honorable?* *How is my lady responding?*
Week 6	Chapters 12, 13 Plan #5 Homework Assignment for Week 7: Write down 3 *minor* life goals, things that you will begin to do this next week to remain at arm's length with the lady in your life this coming week, and implement your plan. Report back your successes to the group next week.	*Am I at "arm's length" in my marriage or serious relationship? Have I tried to live the life of a chivalrous man these past 4 weeks? Where have I succeeded? Failed? How can I improve?* *How is my lady responding?*
Week 7	Chapters 14, 15 Plan #6, Homework Assignment for Week 8: Set 3 new *major* life goals that will help you live a fuller, more chivalrous life with your wife or lady, family, friends, and the world around you. Prepare a "90-Day Action Plan for Chivalrous Living." Write down your plan, and be prepared to present your "90-Day Plan" at the Week 8 Men's Meeting.	*Am I chivalrous according to the Bible? Positives? Negatives? What steps must I take to improve?* *What would need to happen to allow for me/us to move towards exercising a greater degree of chivalry? What barriers or limitations would need to be removed?* *How is my lady responding?*
Week 8	Each man presents his "90-Day Action Plan" to the group, along with his previously planned first steps for chivalrous living, including steps already initiated.	*How can members of the men's group help each other to improve in chivalry?* *How has my lady responded during the eight weeks? What have I learned about her and myself? What steps do I need to take to improve as a chivalrous man? What's my first step? Second step? Third step? Etc.*

To order additional copies of

THE
Chivalrous
MAN
CHIVALRY AND THE GODLY MAN

Have your credit card ready and call

Toll free: (877) 421-READ (7323)

or order online at: www.winepressbooks.com